Equalities and Education in Europe

Equalities and Education in Europe:
Explanations and Excuses for Inequality

By

Alistair Ross, Melinda Dooly
and Nanny Hartsmar

CAMBRIDGE
SCHOLARS

P U B L I S H I N G

Equalities and Education in Europe:
Explanations and Excuses for Inequality,
by Alistair Ross, Melinda Dooly and Nanny Hartsmar

This book first published 2012

Cambridge Scholars Publishing

12 Back Chapman Street, Newcastle upon Tyne, NE6 2XX, UK

British Library Cataloguing in Publication Data
A catalogue record for this book is available from the British Library

Copyright © 2012 by Alistair Ross, Melinda Dooly and Nanny Hartsmar

ISBN (10): 1-4438-3644-3, ISBN (13): 978-1-4438-3644-9

TABLE OF CONTENTS

INTRODUCTION

This book is about inequities in education, primarily in the countries of Europe. Our focus comes not simply from the fact that we are European, and that we best know the educational and social systems of Europe. And although we have worked together on an analysis of educational inequalities in Europe, which we draw on variously through the text of the book, neither is this the reason that we focus on Europe. Our boundary is drawn rather because of the ways in which the countries of Europe, through the European Union, are beginning to address issues of educational disadvantage on a systematic, continent-wide basis. Because of this policy concern, which we discuss further below, we think it is timely to address social and education inequities on the scale of Europe.

In 2005 the European Commission's Department of Education and Culture invited proposals to investigate educational policies and initiatives that had been designed to address social inequalities. Many projects had been tried, in many different countries. What lessons could be drawn? What appeared to work? The authors were part of a team, drawn from seven different countries, that were invited to carry out the study over 2006 to early 2009. We describe, early in this book, what we attempted and how we carried it out: a substantial analysis of the policies of fourteen different countries and seven forms of disadvantage, the analysis of nearly three hundred initiatives, the compilation of over fifty case studies.

But the story does not end there: this is not simply an account, supplemented by other materials and analysis, of practices and policies. The European Commission launches, in the second part of 2012, a significant and major policy initiative of educational initiatives to address disadvantaged groups. The analysis that our study provided has been a contribution to this policy discussions – in the Commission, and between the member states of the Union – that have led to this policy statement. The authors have been involved, at various stages in using the insights we gathered in the project, in helping frame this agenda.

We therefore put forward our analysis – at much greater length, and in a discursive and analytic way not possible in a European Union policy document – of the material on which the policy was in part drawn, and of some of the issues behind the policy and programme. We hope it will be of interest – and of practical and theoretical use – to the policy community and the community of practitioners who will address the Commission's initiative. We undertake research and analysis, of the kind we discuss here, not to simply add to the literature, to contribute to the theory and analysis – but because we also want to make an impact on how education can contribute to positively improving the lives of disadvantaged groups. In various parts of this book we describe and report analyses that suggest that education is doomed to simply reproduce existing social patterns, and that education can do no more than replicate existing social inequities, or even make them worse. This is not our view: we believe that educational policies also have the power to challenge inequalities, and to transform lives.

CHAPTER ONE

THE PROMISE OF EDUCATION

What do we expect education to do? What is its purpose?

These may seem naïve questions, but they lie at the heart of the debate about the nature of inequity in our societies and the future development of social activity. There is no simple and universally agreed answer: different societies have debated and disputed the reasons for why we should teach and learn at least since Aristotle wrote

> ... in modern times there are opposing views about the tasks to be set, for there are no generally accepted assumptions about what the young should learn, either for their own virtue or for the best life; nor is it yet clear whether their education ought to be conducted with more concern for the intellect than for the character or soul ... It is by no means certain whether training should be directed at things useful in life, or at those most conducive to virtue, or at exceptional accomplishments. (Aristotle *The Politics*, Book VIII, Chapter ii: 1337a33)

Do we teach to enhance and develop the individual's intelligence or their social behaviour? Do we spend large sums of money on schooling in order to develop a skilled and able workforce ('the useful things in life'), or to advance socially responsible behaviour ('those most conducive to virtue'), or to support specialised knowledge and progression ('exceptional accomplishments')? Are these competing alternatives, or can some or all be achieved at the same time? These debates are used to pit instrumentalism and utilitarianism against individual development, socio-economic cohesion against socio-political liberties, sciences against humanities. The contested nature of the purpose of education and these ensuing debates are, we will demonstrate in this book, at the heart of the reason why our education systems continue to produce gross social inequalities.

Our concern is with why and how educational systems fail to address equalities of outcome. We write particularly about the context of European educational systems, both because we know most about these systems, and because the European Union has a growing educational policy agenda of its own, but we draw where appropriate on experience and policies from other parts of the world. In particular, as we detail later in this chapter, we draw on our shared research into the policies and practices of fourteen European countries, compiled in a study that was intended to directly address social inequities. The EPASI (Educational Policies Addressing Social Inequity) study investigated the successes and failures of educational policies that set out to address educational inequalities: it is described in more detail in this chapter. Our concern is not with individual inequalities, which form part of the statistical normal distribution of individual differences, but with social inequities, where particular socially-defined groups or sub-sets of the population persistently are shown to achieve less well than the mainstream population. These groups may be defined variously by ethnicity, gender, disability status, socio-economic status, residency, origin, linguistic grouping – and other possibilities – and may sometimes in terms of numbers, rather than power, form the majority. But across Europe we see that there are wide variations in how different groups perform as collectivities in the sphere of education, often despite the presence of particular educational initiatives that are designed to redress these inequities.

Why do these educational inequalities arise and persist in the face of attempts to do away with them? We will argue that to address this issue we need to consider what societies – and their policy makers, educational practitioners, parents and students – think the purpose and possibilities of education to be. What do we expect education to do? What is its promise?

Transformation or Reproduction: two views of the possibilities of Education

The dispute first set out by Aristotle polarises around two belief systems that are frequently set in opposition: that education should preserve cultural and social systems and structures, and that education should be used as an engine for social transformation and change. Teasing out these positions will help illuminate the role of education in social change, and its role in the promotion and reproduction of inequities.

Durkheim characterised education as 'the image and *reflection* of society. It imitates and reproduces the latter in an abbreviated form; it does not create it' (1897: 372; emphasis added). For him, education was the means by which society prepares, within the children, the essential conditions of its very existence. ... the man whom education should realise in us is not man as nature has made him, but as the society wishes to be ... Society draws for us the portrait of the kind of man we should be, and in this portrait all the peculiarities of its organisation come to be *reflected*. (Durkheim 1897: 64 - 5; emphasis added)

This functionalist view is still common: 'all societies have the task of passing on to the next generation the knowledge and skills regarded as particularly worthwhile; ... societies achieve this by means of ... education' (Lawton and Gordon 1996: 10). Although Durkheim's model was not wholly static (Durkheim 1938), it emphasises stability, and sees society as essentially homogeneous. The reflection is mirror-like and results in self-replication. We learn who we are to be: we are what we have learned to be: as Brillat-Savarin put it in a rather different context, 'tell me what you eat: I will tell you who you are' (1825).

By contrast, John Dewey proposed a largely transformative model of education. The school processes should promote social equality, so that 'each individual gets an opportunity to escape from the limitations of the social group in which he was born, and come into living contact with a broader environment' (Dewey, 1916: 20). Education also had a developmental role for the individual: 'it creates a desire for continued growth and supplies the means for making the desire effective in fact' (50). These egalitarian and developmental functions partly derived from Dewey's view of knowledge as something to be constructed by the learner as an active experimenter, provoked into inquiry by the teacher. More recently, John Rawls has similarly argued that education has such egalitarian and developmental functions

Resources for education are not to be allocated solely or necessarily mainly according to their return as estimated in producing trained abilities, but also according to their worth in enriching the personal and social life of citizens, including here the less favoured. (Rawls 1971: 107)

But many observers have argued that, whatever the ambitions the egalitarians and liberals have for education to transform society, this has not happened. Raymond Williams argued that:

the common prescription of education, as the key to change, ignores the fact that the form and content of education are affected, and in some cases determined, by the actual systems of decision and maintenance. (Williams 1961: 120)

Political (decision) and economic (maintenance) structures tend to prescribe the composition of the curriculum and the systems by which it is delivered in ways that minimises the possibility of societal or economic change. Michael Apple develops this further, concluding that schools contribute to inequality because they are intentionally organised to distribute particular kinds of knowledge unequally (Apple 1990: 43). Williams and Apple both hold that the educational systems in Britain and the United States (respectively) are designed to replicate social and economic inequalities.

Education can also be portrayed as the principal engine for social change and transformation. Education, it is argued (particularly by western governments, and by the European Union) will produce social beings or citizens who will challenge xenophobia, sexism, promote human rights, equalities and democracy, who will be able to reason and argue, who will promote sustainable lifestyles, who will be economically literate, environmentally concerned, and be good parents and neighbours. Education will inform people, ensuring that they are literate, numerate, able to use science, speak several languages, and be technologically competent. It will give people the skills, knowledge and competences that make them able to work and sustain themselves and their families' needs. Rather than reflect the old order, education will (or can) act as refracting prism, teasing out a spectrum of attitudes, skills and abilities, altering the direction, form and perspective of the next generation.

But there remains an inherent traditionalism in much educational policy, whatever the extent to which the rhetoric of transformation is employed. Most countries expect the curriculum to maintain and instil what are seen as the country's traditional values and views of its history. Education should support and legitimise current political, social and economic norms. Because all adults have been through an educational process, all see themselves as qualified, by virtue of this experience, to judge what forms and functions education should perform: change becomes difficult when politicians, parents and teachers see proposals for new forms of education as a criticism of the education that made them what they are.

It can also be argued that our educational structures have been created around a model of capitalist production – that there is a correspondence between the nature and organisation of contemporary schooling and the labour requirements of capitalist industrialised economies. The correspondence theory advanced by Bowles and Gintis (1976, 1988) suggests that modern education systems are a simple response to the capitalist system, transmitting technical and social skills (through the overt curriculum) and inculcating discipline and obedience to authority (through the hidden curriculum). The social relations of the means of production correspond to the social relations of schooling, which, they argue, is not a coincidence.

> The school is a bureaucratic order, with hierarchical authority, rule orientation, stratification by 'ability' as well as by age, role differentiation by sex ... and a system of external incentives (marks, promises of promotion, and threat of failure) much like the pay and status in the sphere of work. (Bowles 1973: 357)

It is not simply that schools reproduce the types of personality required by capitalist production ('those at the base of the hierarchy requiring a heavy emphasis on obedience and rules, and those at the top, where discretionary scope is considerable, requiring a greater ability to make decisions on the basis of well-internalised norms' (87)) – this is the very *purpose* of education. Alienation and anomie become the necessary outcomes of this schooling, and are not merely incidental to the incompatibility of the cultures of primary and secondary socialisers (Gramsci 1971; Berger and Luckmann 1966).

From this assertion it follows that schools become mechanisms for cultural distribution and class reproduction: the two are indivisible. The subtle hegemony that the ruling class exercises over the legitimisation of acceptable or valued cultural knowledge is exercised through the control of the knowledge-producing and knowledge-preserving institutions of society (Apple 1990). A particular version or reality is selected and distributed, a social construction picked to serve the interests of a particular segment of society (Mannheim 1936). As Whitty puts it, the question then becomes 'how and why reality comes to be constructed in particular ways, and how and why particular constructions of reality seem to have the power to resist subversion' (Whitty 1974: 125).

Bowles and Gintis examine the connections between technological change, production, capitalist organisation and the educational system. Using US data – though a study of European educational history might produce broadly similar conclusions – they compare the institutional background of the development of modern capitalist systems to the development of the systems of schooling. While they concede that there are some benefits to schooling, such as the elimination of illiteracy and giving access to learning experiences that are intrinsically fulfilling, they argue that the expansion of mass schooling was a response to economic need, not to initiate or promote social reform.

> Schools are destined to legitimate inequality, limit personal development to forms compatible with submission to arbitrary authority, and aid in the process whereby youth are resigned to their fate (Bowles and Gintis 1976: 266)

They point to the explicit links between education's central role in the reproduction of the political structure of capitalist production processes and the legitimisation of the rights vested in property:

> ...education is directly involved in the contradictory articulations of sites in advanced capitalism and is expressed in terms of the property/person dichotomy: education reproduces rights vested in property, while itself [is] organised in terms of rights vested in persons. (Bowles and Gintis 1981: 56)

The inability of education to promote personal development is not because of the content of the curriculum, which has little part to play: it is the form of the educational discourses that determine what is reproduced. As we shall argue later in this volume, this argument is central to the reproduction of inequalities that creates disadvantage for particular groups: it is not what such groups are taught or not taught, but the educational discourse of marginalisation and lowered expectations that determines educational outcomes and inequities.

But Bowles and Gintis also argue that the situation is not necessarily closed. There are contradictions in the system that allow for the possibility of renegotiating more egalitarian consequences, because the dominant – almost the only – mode of discourse provided in schools is that based on natural rights,

> This contradictory position of education explains its dual progressive/reproductive role (promoting equality, democracy, toleration, rationality, inalienable rights on the one hand, while legitimating inequality, authoritarianism, fragmentation, prejudice and submission on the other) and is, in part, a reflection of the stress in liberal discourse on procedure over substance. But it provides as well the tools by means of which it can be transformed into an instrument in the transition to socialism ... the goal of progressive educational reform must be framed in the structural boundaries of liberal discourse, and can be simply expressed as the full democratisation of education. These goals can be divided into two complementary projects: the democratisation of the social relations of

education and the reformulation of the issue of democracy in the curriculum. (Bowles and Gintis 1981: 57)

But this optimism is tempered by what they see as the stronghold of capitalism: they link the development of the American educational system to the need of production; in the early nineteenth century there was a need for a system of training labour. The authors quote educational policy makers of the time who consciously modelled school organisation on the principles of the division of labour in order to meet the needs of the larger employers for an obedient and malleable workforce. They cite an 1854 school board memorandum:

> The object of education is by no means accomplished by mere intellectual instruction. It has other aims of equal if not higher importance. The character and habits are formed for life … of attention, self-reliance, habits of order and neatness, politeness and courtesy … habits of punctuality.

The growth of corporate industry in the late nineteenth century required a more highly differentiated and hierarchically organised labour force, and Bowles and Gintis relate this to the urban school reform movement of the time that led to a domesticated workforce for corporations. The reform was based on standardisation, testing and the bureaucratic tracking of students and the educational system was based on a method that purported to be fair and just in its allocation of individuals to particular social and economic positions, but did so at the behest of larger social and political forces. The same educational system inculcates the population to accept as legitimate the limited roles in society that they are allowed (see also Meyer 1977).

MacDonald has also pointed to the same hierarchical, rule-dominated organisation of schools as a characteristic of the pre-industrial school (MacDonald 1977). She argues that there is a more complex relationship between the educational system and its social setting, better examined by distinguishing the systems for social reproduction from those of cultural reproduction. Though the latter are dependent on the former, cultural reproduction is able to maintain a certain degree of independence.

Pierre Bourdieu's theory of cultural capitalism includes both cultural production and reproduction in schools. The cultural capital, the *habitus* of the middle class, is expressed through its habits of thought, assumptions and complexions, which are particularly expressed through the system of schooling: the school inculcates, partly through the formal curriculum, but particularly through the informal curriculum, 'not so much with particular and particularised schemes of thought as with that general disposition which engenders particular schemes, which may then be applied in particular domains of thought and action' (Bourdieu 1971: 184).

This cultural capital is used as a mechanism to filter pupils to particular positions within the hierarchy of capitalist society. Schools recreate the social and economic hierarchies in the way that they are embedded, using the processes of selection and teaching, judging and comparing performance in these activities against the *habitus* of the middle class, and thus effectively discriminating against all those students who do not have access to this. Dale *et al* summarise Bourdieu's argument thus: 'By taking all children as equal, while implicitly favouring those who have already acquired the linguistic and cultural competencies to handle a middle class culture, schools take as natural what is essentially a social gift, *i.e.* cultural capital' (Dale, Esland and MacDonald 1976: 4). Bourdieu himself argues that 'the cultural capital and the ethos, as they take shape, combine to determine behaviour and attitude to school, which makes up the differential principle of elimination operating for children of different social strata' (Bourdieu 1974: 36). Applying the same cultural criteria in an equal way favours those students who have been previously socialised into the particularly favoured culture:

> ... students from different social milieux owe their ... future to the fact that the selection that they have undergone is not equally severe for all, and that social advantages or disadvantages have gradually been transformed into educational advantages and disadvantages as a result of premature choices which, directly linked to social origin, have duplicated and reinforced their influence. (Bourdieu 1974: 37)

Treating cultural capital in the same way as one would analyse economic capital shows how and why our dominant cultural institutions are organised and operate to allow those who have inherited cultural capital to do better, in just the same way as inherited economic capital favours economic success. 'Like economic capital, cultural capital (good taste, knowledge, ability, language) is unequally distributed through society and by selecting such properties, schools serve to reproduce the distribution of power within the society' (Dale *et al.* 1976: 4). The implications of the unequal distribution will be examined below, when we consider Bourdieu's concepts of Pedagogic Action and Pedagogic Authority.

Bourdieu and Passeron argue that education has a particular function in the transmission of cultural hierarchy: it can reproduce specific realities in particular social classes. They argue that traditional analyses of education tend to separate cultural reproduction from its function of social reproduction, ignoring 'the specific effect of symbolic relations in the reproduction of power relations' (Bourdieu and Passeron 1990: 10). Functional analysts, such as Durkheim, assume that

> the different PAs [Pedagogic Actions] at work in a social formation collaborate harmoniously in reproducing a cultural capital conceived of as the jointly owned property of the whole 'society'. In reality, because they correspond to the material and symbolic interests of groups and classes differently situated within the power relations, these PAs always tend to reproduce the structure of the distribution of cultural capital among those groups or classes, thereby contributing to the reproduction of the social structure. (Bourdieu and Passeron 1990: 11)

This is a very wide-ranging claim. It implies that the 'nature vs. nurture' debate is irrelevant, because we largely do not choose our identity – indeed, we cannot – for 'we receive the cultural identity which has been handed down to us from previous generations. ... As we grow older, we modify the identity we have inherited. The identity is not intrinsic, but the scope for changing it is circumscribed by the social expectations of the group with which we are associated. By our actions we informally reinforce our inherited group affiliation' (Robbins 1991: 174). Bourdieu and Passeron's model claims – insists – that our social identity and our membership of groups are maintained by adopting tastes and lifestyles that serve as identifying images, with no intrinsic value other than to maintain the coherence of the group(s) to which we belong.

We are formally socialised by the system of education. The state establishes a schooling system to give the particular training or instruction necessary for the changing labour market. The schooling system also seeks to build, in the whole population of the state, an identity or association with the state or nation, that is in some ways equivalent or parallel to the group or class affiliation, but on a larger scale. States themselves are artificial or invented constructs (see, eg, Anderson 1991, Hobsbawm and Ranger 1984, Colley 1992) that seek to construct uniform social identities within their synthetic boundaries. Robbins, in his commentary on Bourdieu, argues that while we are taught some things in school that are not necessarily part of this social purpose, for the most part schools are involved in the transmission of arbitrary culture and knowledge. These

> do not help people reconcile their group identity with a national identity, but instead ... distinguish people on supposed merit or ability. The

equalisation of opportunity provided by state education and by the recognition of 'innate' intelligence is a sham. The system simply provides a series of awards or qualifications which, as much as hairstyles, are reinforcements of our previous group identity. The content of courses is such that only those who have already been initiated into the language of school discourses by their earlier socialisation are able to demonstrate 'ability'. Schools which, in response, alter their curricula in order to be able to recognise the merit of students who have been differently socialised, will tend to find that they become marginalised as institutions because they have 'poor standards'. (Robbins 1991: 175)

Michael Young comes to a very similar conclusion in *Knowledge and Control* (1971). Power is unequally distributed in society: the system that allows this is created and maintained at least partly through the transmission of culture. There is a direct relationship between 'those who have access to power and the opportunity to legitimise certain dominant categories, and the processes by which the availability of such categories to some groups enables them to assert power and control over others' (Young 1971: 8).

How does Bourdieu explain the production and legitimisation of cultural goods? He distinguishes the agencies of cultural production – such as theatres and universities – and the cultural agents who produce them – such as writers, academics, artists – that together constitute 'an intellectual field'. Though the field might appear to be neutral, independent and cohesive, within an ethos of intellectual; freedom and autonomy (and thus seeming to make knowledge to be independent of the social context of those who produce it), Bourdieu argues that those who work in a particular cultural field have acquiesced to the demand that they should adopt a particular cultural code. This code determines the categories of thought, perception and meaning that constitute and order the way that the cultural agent perceives reality – in other words, their *habitus*. This makes educational institutions not simply guides to 'official' culture, but agents that reinforce the social groups that support their choice of approved culture. The action of the educational establishments (schools and universities) is to conserve and reproduce this culture, ensuring that individuals designated as 'successful' have the specific set of values, tastes and thoughts. The organisation and validation of knowledge is more important than the mere content of knowledge. It is not *what knowledge* that is important; it is *how knowledge* is validated that is significant and how its power-forming characteristics are used.

Culture both classifies knowledge and, in its power-validating mode, classifies the classifiers, determining those who have the power of cultural legitimation and those who do not. In *Reproduction in Education, Society and Culture* (1990) Bourdieu and Passeron describe this process of Pedagogic Action as 'symbolic violence, insofar as it is the imposition of a cultural arbitrary by an arbitrary power (5). Schools and universities have the Pedagogic Authority designating them as 'fit to transmit that which they transmit, [and] entitled to impose its reception and test its inculcation by means of socially approved ... sanctions' (20). This control of the reproduction of culture means (as MacDonald summarises) 'the culture which the school transmits is not therefore a collective cultural heritage, but rather the culture of the dominant class' (1977: 40). Education controls cultural reproduction, and thus is one of the principal mechanisms to reproduce the class structure. Bourdieu observes that this is a process that is very well-suited for contemporary states that deny the hereditary tradition of power and privilege.

> Among all the solutions put forward throughout history to the problem of the transmission of power and privilege, there surely does not exist one that is better concealed ... than the solution which the educational system provided by contributing to the reproduction of class relations and by concealing ... that it fulfils this function. (Bourdieu 1971: 72)

Bourdieu constructs his notion of cultural capital in terms of the reproduction of a class system. In this book, we argue that it performs the same role in the reproduction and preservation of a much wider range of social inequities, positioning ethnic and linguistic minorities, those with disabilities, women, some religious minorities and others as necessarily inferior, lacking the necessary designated cultural capital. The role of cultural capital is acquired by the child from their family, through particular linguistic and social competencies and expectations ('style', 'manners', 'know-how'), and these skills and expectations give the child the ability to read, or not read, the code of the dominant culture, so that they can access, decode and accumulate this culture.

This culture and expectation can be contrasted with the range of cultures held by other social groups, such as working class culture and the various cultures of minority ethnic groups and languages, for example. Children outside the privileged class or social category, who have not acquitted the specific skills for handling the privileged cultural capital from their family, or whose families and cultural leaders expect their children to be incapable of successfully directing their skills at decoding the dominant culture, will begin school deprived of the ability to recognise and respond to the dominant culture that the school represents, transmits and arbitrates upon. Privileged children arrive inured in the *habitus* to respond to academic training, and the expectation that they will do so. The others are positioned on the wrong side of a segregating cultural rift, that divides school culture and discourse from their own culture and everyday knowledge, and that expects them not to be able to bridge this. The dominant culture is described and delimited in symbols that are imposed in a way that subordinate groups are unable to decipher them, and transmitting the expectation that they will not be able to successfully learn to do so. Symbolic violence is the power 'to impose meanings ... as legitimate by concealing the power relations which are the basis of its force' (Bourdieu and Passeron 1990: 4).

Inequity and institutional discrimination in Education

Nevertheless, there is a rhetoric that education can be a potent engine for social change and transformation. There is an awareness of inequalities, and governments in Europe, and the European Union. For example, on inequalities in education in gender, EU Commissioner Androulla Vassilio introduces a Eurydice report on gender differences in educational outcomes:

Gender equality has long been a major goal at European level. Since the 1970s, various directives have laid the foundation of equal treatment and equal opportunities in Europe. However, despite the existence of comprehensive legislative frameworks, gender equality is yet to be achieved. Although women form the majority of students and university graduates in most countries, they still earn less and have lower employment rates than men. With regard to education and training, gender differences persist in both attainment and choice of courses of study. (Eurydice 2009: 3)

The report goes on to identify the policy directions and exhortations across European governments towards this.

On the educational achievements of migrants, the Commission has published a Green Paper (European Commission 2008) on aspects of migration and education, that highlights the variations between outcomes in different countries. In all countries both first and second generation migrants perform less well than 'native' students, and there is also wide variation between different countries in their success at closing the gap – in most countries there is only minimal improvement between generations, with substantial differences between the second generation scores and the 'native' scores, and in at least two countries there is a *fall* in attainment – second generation pupils perform less well than their parents had performed (see below, figure 3.1, p 58).

What these two – and other reports – identify is inequalities between groups, which is the principal focus of this book. It is important to distinguish inequalities between individuals and inequalities between groups. There will always be some form of inequality between how individuals perform and succeed in many aspects of life. It is, of course, important that resources are given to ensuring that significant inequalities are minimised, by giving additional support to disadvantaged individuals, and even more important that societies recognise that everyone has equality in terms of human rights, dignity and esteem. But our concern here is inequity between groups: that is, where an identifiable population has an overall distribution of performance significantly different from the distribution of performance of the mean population. There are aspects of inequalities that may apply to both individuals and groups: Burchardt and Vizard (2008) distinguished three - inequality of outcome (that is, inequalities in central or valuable aspects of life that are achieved), inequalities in autonomy (that is, varying degrees of independence in decision making about lives, the realities of choice and control), and inequalities in processes (that is, differential subjection through discrimination or disadvantage by others).

If a group within the population are achieving a less favourable distribution of educational outcomes than the majority of the population, then we argue here that it is reasonable to make an initial presumption that there have been inequalities in social and educational policies. The objective of policy should be to ensure that all groups within society have similar profiles of attainment. To achieve this may require differential (unequal) treatment for a particular group. The onus should be on those responsible for educational policy to demonstrate that all necessary policies are in place to achieve this. It is useful here to develop the principle set out in the Macpherson Report (UK Home Office 1999), which examined institutional process within a UK police force around the racist murder of Stephen Lawrence. The report defined the term 'institutional racism' to refer to

> the collective failure of an organisation to provide an appropriate and professional service to people because of their colour, culture or ethnic origin. It can be seen or detected in processes, attitudes and behaviour which amount to discrimination through unwitting prejudice, ignorance,

thoughtlessness and racist stereotyping which disadvantage minority
ethnic people. (§ 6.34)

In other words, it is the outcome of policy and practice that is significant,
not the intention. In respect of this study, the fact that various groups
continue to suffer educational disadvantage, despite policy initiatives to
counter this, suggests that whatever the intentions, educational systems
institutionally discriminate against the disadvantaged. The term educational
institutional inequality might be usefully employed to identify the
collective failure of an educational institution or set of institutions to
provide appropriate educational services to a minority group of the
population because of their social, cultural, linguistic or behavioural
characteristics. This can be detected in educational policies and practices
that amount to discrimination through 'unwitting prejudice, ignorance,
thoughtlessness and stereotyping' which leads to the group as a whole to
achieve a lower set of educational outcomes than the majority population.

The European Dimension

Ambitions to address inequity often sit uneasily with other policy
initiatives and with deeper ideologies. Educational attainment has become
increasingly competitive, as instrumental reasons are used to justify
educational policies and to drive parental and national ambitions.
Examining first international competition, the development of scales and
league tables that have followed the introduction of the Programme for the
International Student Assessment (PISA) has lead to individual
governments fretting about international rankings, asserting that these are
closely related to eventual economic performance (on very little evidence
of a correlation). In turn, the European Union has set itself the target of
maintaining (or improving) Europe's comparative educational ranking.
The Lisbon European Council meeting of heads of government concluded

> The European Union is confronted with a quantum shift resulting from
> globalisation and the challenges of a new knowledge-driven economy.
> These changes are affecting every aspect of people's lives and require a
> radical transformation of the European economy. (European Union 2000,
> § 1)

A strategic target was set: 'to become the most competitive and dynamic
knowledge-based economy in the world' (§ 5, and as part of this agreed
that

Europe's education and training systems need to adapt both to the demands of the knowledge society and to the need for an improved level and quality of employment. They will have to offer learning and training opportunities .... (§ 25)

The Commission has developed these strategies, and recent documents stress that education should be seen in economic terms, designed to create a competitive economy. A working document of 2007 (*Towards more knowledge-based policy and practice in education and training*) sets out the agenda:

The 2000 Lisbon European Council identified knowledge as the key to future growth, jobs and social cohesion in the EU. We need policies that reinforce this knowledge base. Education and training are a prerequisite for a fully functioning 'knowledge triangle' (education – research – innovation). Member States and the EU institutions need to use evidence-based policy and practice, including robust evaluation instruments, to identify which reforms and practices are the most effective, and to implement them most successfully. The 2006 Spring European Council Conclusions stressed the need for an evaluation culture .... Education and training have a critical impact on economic and social outcomes. Ineffective, misdirected or wasteful education policies incur substantial financial and human costs. It is therefore essential that investment in education ... is as efficient and effective as possible. (European Commission 2007: 1)

The agenda for both research – the creation of cultural capital – and education – the reproduction of cultural capital and of social structure are now embedded in this neo-liberal competitive model. European Union research is planned 'in the broader context of the various policy initiatives and the co-ordination process that form part of the Lisbon strategy, notably in the fields of economic and employment policies, enterprise policy, education and training policy, and the internal market strategy' (European Commission 2010: 7).

This is not only competition on an international level. There are similar competitive motivations in the way that individuals now view education. Many individual parents and students view education as a competition that is a zero-sum game: that is, there are inexorably winners and losers. It is not merely that if one child wins, another loses: the point is that the other child *must* lose in order for education to have been successful. The commodification of education, its location in a competitive market, and the dominant discourse of instrumentalism have turned education into a game that requires losers in order to be successful. But there are other

European imperatives: for example, in a European Union Council Recommendation of 2009 (EU 2009) considering the education of children with a migrant background, it was recognised that

> Education has a key role to play not only in ensuring that children with a migrant background can fulfil their potential to become well-integrated and successful citizens, but also in creating a society which is equitable, inclusive and respectful of diversity. Yet many such children continue to fare less well in terms of educational outcomes, and issues related to racial and ethnic discrimination and to social exclusion are to be found in all parts of the European Union. The presence of significant numbers of learners with migrant backgrounds in many Member States thus presents a number of challenges – but also valuable opportunities – for their education systems. (EU 2009: 2, Recognition §4)

These are opportunities for the educational policies and structures of the European countries to change and transform, and challenges for them to counter social inertia and the reproduction of social norms and inequities.

We suggest that education as an activity can do any, all or none of the above. It has a potential to transform and to change society – in what we call a 'positive' way – developing social justice, minimising inequalities, promoting human rights, dignities and capacities. But although these values are notionally subscribed to by the great majority of people in Europe, the same people often use education in practice to maintain inequalities and injustices. They, wittingly or unwittingly, use education to explain or excuse inequity.

This book sets out to explain how this happens, and how education could seize the argument and act to transform. It tries to show how denials and excuses are used to evade the issue.

An analysis based on Equalities

We began our work together in this area in 2007 when we collaborated on a study for the European Commission that investigated the successes and failures of educational policies that set out to address educational inequalities. EPASI, as it became known (Educational Policies Addressing Social Inequity), reported in early 2009 (www.epasi.eu). Partners from seven countries systematically examined some 280 projects in fourteen different European Union countries, and teased out the ways in which educational inequity was conceptualised in each of these countries' policies. We are grateful to all the members of the study team for their discussions, insights and debates, but this book does not attempt to reproduce the findings of that study, and we alone are responsible for the arguments and conclusions that we set out here. That study focused our attention on both the lack of lasting success of so many policies, and on what appeared to us to be the very muddled theorisation of inequity that was being applied by so many educational policy makers. This book is directed at these issues, rather than those underlying EPASI, but nevertheless we have continued to draw on the experience of this study, and here acknowledge our debt to our collaborators (Box 1).

Box 1

Those involved in the EPASI Project

Educational Policies Addressing Social Inequity

London Metropolitan University, Institute of Policy Studies in Education (UK): Alistair Ross (Project Coordinator, UK Team leader); Carole Leathwood; Sarah Minty; Marie-Pierre Moreau; Nicola Rollock and Katya Williams

Katholieke Hogeschool Zuid-West-Vlaanderen (Belgium): Hugo Verkest (BE Team leader); Evelien Geurts; Bie Lambrechts and Andries Termote.

Univerzita Hradec Králové (Czech Republic): Pavel Vacek (CZ Team leader); Daniela Vrabcova; Jan Lašek and Michaela Pišová.

Montpellier 111 - Université Paul Valéry (France): Richard Étienne (FR Team leader); Bénédicte Gendron; Chantal Étienne and Pascal Tozzi.

Panepistimio Patron / Πανεπιστημιο Πατρων (Greece): Julia Spinthourakis (GR Team leader); Eleni Karatzia-Stavlioti; Georgia-Eleni Lempesi; Ioanna Papadimitriou and Chrysovalante Giannaka.

Universitat Autònoma of Barcelona (Spain): Melinda Dooly (ES Team leader); Claudia Vallejo; Miquel Essomba and Virginia Unamuno, with Ferran Ferrer.

Malmö högskola (Sweden): Nanny Hartsmar (SE Team leader); Meta Margareta Cederberg; Svante Lingärde and Jan Nilsson.

Our book attempts to set out an argument that educational policy makers need to reconceptualise what is meant by inequality, reformulate their characterisations and explanations of why some groups do not achieve as well as others educationally; and above all, redirect the focus of programmes that are designed to address inequity towards the population as a whole, rather than to direct isolated focus on particular communities.

Just as the basis for social inequity and educational disadvantage is not a straightforward, transparent cause-and-effect process, the discussion of these issues is, at times, circular and complex. This is reflected in the following chapters: recurrent themes emerge, although they are approached from different perspectives. The question of underlying ideologies is interrogated from an economic perspective as well as a discursive perspective, for instance, and from the point of view of the individual as well as on a more 'macro' society level. Chapter two begins our discussion about equality and equity by considering different economic approaches that have been applied to explain and interpret these notions. However, further on we argue that it is important to distinguish other arguments for addressing group inequalities (e.g. the human rights argument) from economic ones, since the premise taken may alter significantly subsequent educational policies and practices that arise.

The topic of educational opportunity is another topic that is revisited through the chapters – arguments that equal opportunity is sufficient for overcoming the radical structural inequalities is interrogated from an economic perspective, a discursive perspective and a socio-political perspective in the different chapters. The concept of 'meritocracy' is also a recurrent theme: it is discussed in detail in chapter three but, inevitably, it comes up again in a discursive analysis of how disadvantaged groups are categorised or labelled and the consequences of such actions. Throughout the book, we look at different reasons which have been advanced to explain or justify inequalities in education – chapter three provides an overview of reasons that have been employed in recent decades concerning reasons that specific groups have lower achievement records. Chapter four examines these 'excuses and evasions' in detail and chapter five considers them from the perspective of socially constructed discourse.

Thus, starting from an economic perspective, we examine what is meant by equality, and offer some theorisation of inequity. Why do societies make some of their members unequal, and create 'others' who are destined not to achieve and succeed. We discuss the social consequences of inequalities, and theories of social justice, linking these in the European context to the arguments for a social model for Europe. In particular, we look at how setting up education as a competitive enterprise – student against student, school against school, nation against nation – leads to classification and grading that divides groups as well as individuals into achievers and non-achievers, successes and failures. And from this comes a whole rhetorical barrage of explanations and excuses for inequity. Education creates and sustains inequalities, and a set of discourses that justify its existence.

The following chapter looks at how analysts have sought to explain and sometimes justify educational inequities. Categories of inequities have been created, based on social, political, cultural and psychological theories, and sets of underachieving groups have been defined and 'explained'. In may cases, taking a progressive and interventionists approach, policy-makers have then set out to address each underachieving group, explicitly intending to remedy the perceived deficiencies of the group. This remedialisation of social categories, we argue, often tends to exacerbate social difference, pathologising particular groups, and may often exacerbate educational underachievement.

In chapter four we examine the evasions and excuses that the educational policy community employs to explain the failure of these remedialisation policies. One set of explanations are based on denial: disadvantaged groups don't really exist, only disadvantaged individuals; opportunities for success are equalised, to ensure 'the playing field is level' (the metaphors of competition revealing so much); the emphasis on the provision of equal opportunities being sufficient to deal with the issue and to evade any responsibility to address any subsequent inequalities in attainment. A second set of explanations are used to excuse the lack of success of these programmes. There are other policy initiatives that may counter equality initiatives, perpetuating inequities; policies that either avoid identifying underlying social and economic structural inequities, or shift the blame for educational policy failures on to these inequities. The consequences of these excuses is that everyone sees inequitable educational outcomes as an inevitability: members of the socially disadvantaged groups, members of successful groups, and above all the students see themselves as predestined educational failures.

In the following chapter we then examine the dangers in policies that focus on identifying and isolating underachieving groups. We argue that while the identification of groups at risk is necessary, because we need to quantify the inequity, to target resources and programmes, and to assess the effectiveness (if any) of the impact of such targeting, this type of intervention also serves to polarise society and schools. The 'achieving' majority perceive the 'other' groups as underachieving, and view their presence as a threat to the standards achieved by their own children. Stereotyping difference is too often seen as the inevitable consequence: neighbourhoods segregate, groups become isolated, and expectations are lowered. Efforts that are made to empower such groups and to involve them in the solutions may even lead to them being blamed for lack of success.

In chapter six we suggest that many educational policies in this field have been misdirected. Instead of identifying groups as failing, and directing programmes that are simply concerned with remedial action directed at rectifying deficiencies, we should also seek to work with the majority or mainstream community (and with other minority communities) to redress stereotyping, misconceptions, and above all to raise expectations of success. We argue that raising expectations is critical – not only the expectations of the students themselves, and of their parents and communities, and not only the expectations of the teachers who work with them, but fundamentally the expectations of the whole society, of all members of the society, need to be changed. This is not a straightforward process: as has been already argued in this chapter, and will be revisited later in the book, many people regard education as a competition, and one which is a zero-sum game competition. Raising the achievement of underachieving groups and individuals is all too often seen as threatening the achievement of other children ('our children'), because differentials in achievement will be lowered.

But we argue that transforming educational outcomes for disadvantaged groups *is* a task that education can perform: education does have the promise to transform and to create equity, given the structures, direction, policy and will. We hope to explain this in the following chapters. To begin, we must discuss what we mean by equality and equity.

CHAPTER TWO

WHAT DO WE MEAN BY EQUALITY?

Why do inequality and inequity in education matter? To examine this, we need to examine what is meant by equality, and offer some theorisation of inequity. There are a variety of potential definitions of the two terms. Generally, equality is seen as a condition where individuals have the same quantity of a particular good or service, or the same rank or status, or are valued the same. Thus individuals can be conceived of as being unequal in terms of wealth, but be seen as having equal human rights - although many would argue that inequities in material resources make it very difficult to attain equalities in other spheres: it is sometimes said that in England 'justice is open to all; like the Ritz hotel' - a saying variously attributed to Lord Birkett or Mr Justice Mathew (Willey 2010) that means that while the system of law is theoretically available to everyone, in reality access is limited to those who can afford to pay for it. The concept of equity takes on this disjuncture: it considers the social justice implications of the distribution of a service (in this case, education) in respect of fairness, justice and impartiality (Holsinger and Jacob 2009).

Before looking specifically at equality and equity in terms of education, it might be useful to first review the various debates and positions that are held about economic equity and equality.

Equality and equity in income and wealth

We will first briefly review the principle classic and contemporary positions on inequalities of wealth and income, before turning to arguments about the justification and value of attempting to counter such inequalities.

The *libertarian* would not generally have a perspective on inequalities in wealth or resources, but would argue that equality under the law is the only fundamentally necessary equality (Boaz 1998, Quinton 1995). They would argue that inequalities in a society are the basis for cooperation and interdependence: equality under the law ensures that society as a whole maximises its overall wealth, because social institutions are not allowed to prevent any individual from maximising their talents, abilities and individual prosperity. Some libertarians argue that taxation is a governmental mechanism to force the redistribution of wealth (eg Nozick 1974), and ideally a society should not allow such force. But in practice, such *classical liberals* admit that in most societies the economic inequalities are based on the historically forced appropriation of property, and that force would be properly required to redistribute this – but, Nozick argues, to compensate for the original use of force, not to achieve any levelling or equality.

John Rawls (1971) uses his difference principle (which will be discussed in more detail with reference to education in the following section) to assert that inequalities in wealth are only permissible if they act to improve society as a whole, including the least well-off. This has been interpreted by some – such as Friedman (1990, 2002) – as supporting capitalism, because, it can be argued, that the increased wealth and productivity that capitalism allows will, at least theoretically, benefit all ('including the least well-off'). Friedman, like Hayek (1976), argues that political freedom is the most necessary freedom: if governments attempt to redistribute wealth in pursuit of economic equality, political freedoms will be lost.

Thus Rawls asks what would be a just distribution in a society, and what kinds of inequality might be justified, and to what extent. He concludes that only those inequalities that benefit the least advantaged can be allowed, such as when particular inequalities of power or wealth produce greater wealth and advantage for all members of a society. Nozick's response to this is that inequalities arise from individual differences, and that these resources are thus legitimately held by individuals, and there is no collective social right to redistribute these. Nozick argues from the perspective of individual's rights: for him, justice is not about equalities or inequalities, but about the right of the individual to possess what he or she has acquired. In answer to these arguments, Wade (2005) effectively summarises critiques of the liberal stance: they

> … emphasize that inequality is, first, an inevitable consequence of respecting property rights and, second, a necessary condition for effort and risk-taking and thereby for efficiency. For all these reasons, liberals tend to dismiss questions about the growing gap between rich and poor as 'the politics of envy.' They say that public policy should not worry about income inequality provided it results from 'fair' market processes—and

provided it does not reach the point where popular resentment of great wealth threatens the liberal order (Wade 2005: 13)

In complete contradistinction, a broad *Marxist* perspective would be to link economic inequalities to political or power inequalities (eg Anderson 1984). To be politically equal in reality, members of a society must have more or less equal wealth, and resources would be distributed on the basis of need, rather than ability to produce, the ownership of property, or inherited wealth. A pure Marxist perspective would be that if the means of production are owned by all, and managed to maximise their use, rather than to maximise profits, then all would have equal power in the workplace. The Marxist-Leninist perspective would be that workers would, for a limited period, need to be paid according to their labour, rather than their need.

The *meritocratic* argument, which will be analysed in more detail in chapter three, is that each individual's wealth should be directly related to their ability or contribution – their merit. Economic inequality is thus merely a reflection of individual effort and ability, and this is a social benefit, encouraging effort and application. But, as will be shown, one generation's accumulation of wealth through ability and skill becomes the next generation's inherited wealth (Giddens and Diamond 2005).

Social justice arguments are based on the view that wealth and incomes are in practice arbitrary and based on present or past violations, and that they therefore need to be redistributed

> The steady rise of inequalities in the distribution of wealth ... requires asset redistribution, the democratisation of market capitalism, and the containment of excessive accumulation of wealth by a few individuals. Just as [earlier] social policy drew a distinction between the 'deserving' and 'undeserving' poor, these categories might be applied to the concentration of wealth. The accumulation of wealth is excessive and unjust where it arises not from hard work and risk-taking enterprise, but from 'brute luck' factors such as rising returns on property and land. Inheritance itself is a form of brute-luck inequality, enabling citizens to share in the social product while violating the principle of reciprocity: if one citizen enjoys the fruits of another's labour, a good or service should be provided in return. The case for liberty does not, therefore, defeat the case for taxation of wealth transfers. (Giddens and Diamond, 2005: 203)

Such claims are often backed with arguments that inequalities of wealth and income are socially divisive and weaken communities. Wilkinson and Pickett (2009) argue more than this: to them, unequal societies lead to not only more crime and social problems, but to poorer health, life expectancy and education for all, including the most wealthy: their evidence in respect of education will be examined below. Others, such as Alesina (Alesina and Rodrik 1994; Alesina and Perotti 1996) argue that inequality impacts on a society's sense of well-being and happiness. Inequalities in wealth almost inevitably lead to inequalities in political power: just as economic poverty is a relative concept, not an absolute, so the distribution of political power is also relative (Giddens and Diamond, 2005). It is harder to participate in a social democracy if one is economically less powerful.

A rather different, but essentially related, argument against economic inequality is advanced in the *capabilities approach* of Amartya Sen (1985, 1992). Opportunities for economic (and social and political) development are of no value if one lacks the capabilities to properly take full advantage of them. Sen argues that economic inequality is a form of incapability: without political freedom, social opportunities and security, people are unable to enjoy what they value doing or to pursue the goals they value. Wealth and income, Sen argues, are not ends in themselves, but a means to enjoy other ends, but if social structures (such as ignorance, government oppression, lack of financial resources, or false consciousness) deprive the individual of the capacity to maximise their earnings, they cannot achieve these. Without these capabilities, inequalities will increase: poverty is the deprivation of capabilities such as the ability to have a long and healthy life and to participate in economic, social and political life.

These different positions predicate different responses: a typical neo-liberal response would be to argue that:

> There is little evidence that high levels of income inequality lead down a slippery slope to the destruction of democracy and rule by the rich. The unequal political voice of the poor can be addressed only through policies that actually work to fight poverty and improve education. Income inequality is a dangerous distraction from the real problems: poverty, lack of economic opportunity, and systemic injustice. (Wilkinson 2009: 1)

Against the above argument, those who argue for capabilities and social justice would point out:

> ... the social consequences of economic inequality are ... seldom ... positive. The case for inequality seems to rest entirely on the claim that it promotes efficiency, and the evidence for that claim is thin. ... If you are a hard-core Rawlsian who thinks that society's sole economic goal should be to improve the position of the least advantaged, European experience

suggests that limiting inequality can benefit the poor. If you are a hard-core utilitarian, European experience suggests - though it certainly does not prove - that limiting inequality lowers consumption. But European experience also suggests that lowering inequality reduces consumption partly by encouraging people to work fewer hours, which many Europeans see as a good thing. If you care more about equal opportunity for children than about consumption among adults, limiting economic inequality among parents probably reduces disparities in the opportunities open to their children. (Jencks 2001: 49)

Wade also takes on some of the empirical evidence about differences in economic quality in various economically developed countries. He points to one particular region in Europe – Scandinavia - which has much lower after-tax income inequality than most other such countries, which has also, he argues

'shown better economic and social performance than both the rest of Europe and the United States by most of the important yardsticks—economic growth, labor productivity, research and development investment, product and service markets, performance in high technology and telecommunications sectors, rates of employment, physical and social infrastructure, and income equality' (Wade 2005: 29).

Despite this, the European Commission appears obsessed with the model of the United States.

There are two broad arguments for the need to address – or attempt to address – economic inequalities. The World Bank World Development Report 2006 (World Bank 2005) focussed on equity and development: it highlighted the interaction between different forms of inequality, suggesting that inequality of opportunity is wasteful, and that equity has an intrinsic value. In the on-line discussion organised by the World Bank that followed publication, many participants argued that inequality was important both because it violates basic human rights and because it hinders growth and poverty reduction. One participant said 'It is crucial to argue solidly that inequality matters a lot from different points of view, [so fighting it becomes] more and more accepted by everyone.' (World Bank 2006). Sen's capability arguments are frequently employed to explore how inequity is maintained and even accentuated. Many participants in the World Bank discussion agreed

that inequalities in financial markets reduce economic efficiency and provided examples of how expanded access to credit has helped poor people – self-help groups in India, government provision of housing that could be used as collateral in Portugal. However, several noted that unequal access to financial markets is only one constraint, often not the most binding; poor people often also lack access to markets, land, capital, and knowledge. Moreover, lack of access to financial markets is often due to discrimination. ... [other participants] tended to agree that inequality tends to induce the capture of institutions by a powerful elite, which in turn stifles growth and poverty reduction, and mentioned examples from their own countries. Several noted that capture of state institutions is not limited to developing countries. (World Bank 2006)

We argue here that it is important to distinguish the human rights argument for addressing group inequalities from the instrumental economic argument that inequalities are wasteful. Policies that are designed to address inequalities from one of these premises may differ substantially from those policies based on the alternative argument.

'Does inequality matter?' implies that inequality is treated as the independent variable. The question can be answered in terms of moral or intrinsic values. We can present a moral case that the magnitude of inequalities in the world today is simply 'unacceptable,' especially in light of the rather small cost to the rest of the world's population of substantially raising up the bottom tail of the distribution (eliminating extreme poverty). The question can also be answered in more instrumental terms, to do with the effects of higher or lower inequality on other things. If we do not like (some of) these effects, we have some basis for concluding that, yes, inequality does matter, and public policy should aim to reduce it, both between countries and within countries where it is relatively high—because lower inequality benefits other variables that we care about. (Wade 2005: 26-27)

Equality and equity in education

Economic equality is, however, different from educational equality. While a society might be able to ensure real equality of educational opportunity ('real' being more than simple availability and access), it cannot create a system in which everyone achieves the same benefits from that education: there is (or appears to be) an inevitable distribution of educational attainments. This is one reason why, we argue, discussions about educational policies and educational equity should focus on equality of outcomes between different social groups. We argue that there is no reputable evidence that any social group – be it females, those of African origin, those with disabilities, or members of the working class – are less able to achieve the same educational standards as those who most current educational systems brand as more capable (white, able-bodied, middle class males, etc.).

Farrell (1999) suggests that equity focuses on the social justice of how educational provision is distributed in practice (thus following Bronfenbrenner (1973), but points out that this will often be constructed very differently from different group or sub-group perspectives. Gewirtz, Ball and Bowe (1995) refer to educational equity as being a values-based system, while equality is 'fact'-based. Amartya Sen (1992) posed a series of questions about equality and equity: equality, he argued, is a particularly complex question because human diversity is such that there will always be competing values and need, and thus competing claims to equality. Distributing any kind of resources is inevitably normative: 'the answer we give to equality of what, will not only endorse quality in that chosen space, but will have far reaching consequences on the distributional patterns in other spaces' (Sen 1992: 21). So the implications of what becomes a normative decision about equality requires some form of collective agreement about what is valuable, and who should get it, in a way that is equitable (Mulderigg 2007)

Sen illustrated the dilemma more recently (2009), when he set out the differences in a parable-like form. He contrasts three children's competing claims for ownership of a flute. Anne is the only one of the three who can play the instrument; Bob, unlike the other two children, who are rich, asks for it on the grounds of distributive fairness; whilst Carla's claim rests on the grounds that she had, over many months, made the flute (Sen 2009: 12 – 15). Bob's claim would be supported by economic egalitarians, seeking to reduce differences between the (economic) means of people. Carla's claim is both libertarian and recognises the labour theory of value. Anne's claim is based on hedonistic utilitarianism, and on the principle of not wasting an asset. But, as Sen sets out, utilitarian, egalitarian and libertarians will all recognise the dilemma of what is equitable, and acknowledge that there is some validity in the other claimants' arguments:

> It is not easy to brush aside as foundationless any of the claims based respectively on the pursuit of human fulfilment, or removal of poverty, or entitlement to enjoy the products of one's own labour. The different resolutions all have serious arguments in support of them, and we may not be able to identify, without sore arbitrariness, any of the alternative arguments as being the one that must inevitably prevail (Sen 2009: 14)

It was in response to Sen's 1992 question 'Equality of what?' that Grisay (1984) suggested four aspects of equality in education, that might together be seen as constituting a form of equity: these are the principles of natural equality, equality of access, equality of outcome or achievement, and equality of treatment. We shall be basing much of our later discussion on equities and inequities on the distinctions between access, achievement and treatment, and in particular to the equitable treatment of different groups. While we can, in theory, require and insist that individuals have natural equality, particularly in terms of educational access and treatment in educational settings, there will not be equality of outcomes for all individuals. But when we turn to inequities between groups, we can, as noted in the previous chapter, expect that the attainment of groups to be broadly the same – and if they are not, to consider this to be a *prima fascia* case of educational inequity.

Sen's particular contribution has been the concept of capability as a measure of equality. The fairness of a government, he argued, should be assessed by the capabilities of their citizens, rather that the opportunities that may be made available to them, which remain theoretical opportunities or rights if citizens do not have the capability to exercise them (Sen 1980). He argues the right to vote is not real, if citizens lack the capacity to vote – the education to understand the process, the possibility of getting to the polling station. Sen has led the critiques of the economic model that self-interest drives all human behaviour.

John Rawls' work, set out in *A Theory of Justice* (1971) established two essential principles for social justice to be effective: firstly, each person should have an equal right to the most extensive scheme of equal basic liberties that is compatible with a similar scheme of liberties for others. These would include the traditional liberties of political activity, property, speech, assembly, conscience, and so on. The second principle he puts forward concerns how social and economic inequity is to be dealt with: he argues that they should be so ordered that they are to be of the greatest benefit to the least-advantaged members of society (which he terms 'the difference principle'), and there must be equality of opportunity to all to participate in holding office and positions (Rawls, 1971: 303). But he argues that this is not a principle of redressing inequities.

> It does not require society to try to even out handicaps as if all were expected to compete on a fair basis. But the difference principle would allocate resources in education, say, so as to improve the long-term expectations of the least favored. If this end is attained by giving more

attention to the better endowed, it is permissible; otherwise not. And in making this decision, the value of education should not be assessed only in terms of economic efficiency and social welfare. Equally if not more important is the role of education in enabling a person to enjoy the culture of his society and to take part in its affairs, and in this way to provide for each individual a secure sense of his own worth (Rawls 1971: 101)

He is claiming here that basic or primary goods should be equally distributed, and inequalities in this only tolerated if this would improve the lot of those who are worst-off under that distribution in comparison with the previous, equal, distribution. Chances of birth and of inborn talents, he asserts, should not determine life chances. The second element of his difference principle – equality of opportunity, is fundamental in that it demands that all should have the opportunity to acquire all those skills on which merit is judged. Specifically, he argues that

resources for education are not to be allocated solely or necessarily mainly according to their return as estimated in producing trained abilities, but also according to their worth in enriching the personal and social lives of citizens, including here the less favoured. As a society progresses, the latter consideration becomes increasingly more important. (Rawls 1971: 107)

The European Union's educational policy is somewhat ambiguous on issues of equality and equity. In the previous chapter we referred to the increasing instrumentalist agenda that the Union and the Commission are determining for education: the focus of many (but not all) initiatives is to develop education in order to maximise the employability of young people. This in itself is not necessarily an agenda that ignores inequity: if there are substantial numbers of young people who are unprepared for the labour market, this will create relative poverty and thus lead to structural inequity. Yet there is within this a focus on competitive educational systems across Europe, that also differentiate and lead to inequalities. This is a perhaps inevitable contradiction, that reflects the tension within the entire 'European Project' – it seeks to create a single market, with all the inequities in wealth, status, possessions and consumption that stem from market forces, alongside the establishment of common and enforceable political, social, economic and cultural rights for individuals, with the values of equity that these imply.

Many aspects of the competitive models of education that are encouraged in many contemporary educational policies in Europe encourage market forces to determine what is seen as educational success. Schools are set against schools in the competition of league tables that largely ignore the social context in which individual schools find themselves; and pupils are set against pupils in the accumulation of credits and grades that will differentiate them in both the labour market and in access to opportunities for post-compulsory education. PISA and other comparative analyses of performance encourage international league tables in particular subjects, in the rather strange presumption that these will have a bearing on a nation's economic performance.

Table 2.1 compares the PISA scores and rankings, and the GDP per capita rates, for 24 European countries. There is strikingly little relationship between any of the scores for mathematics, the sciences and reading and the GDP per person. Moreover, while there is an eight-fold difference between the highest income country and the lowest, the highest scoring countries in PISA only score between 14 and 18% higher than the lowest scoring countries. The suggestion that such a low relative difference in scores could relate to such a much greater level of difference between average income per person is rather problematic.

The average income per person for a country gives an indication of national differences, but says nothing about the distribution of incomes, and thus inequalities and inequities, within a country. To do this, the Gini coefficient is a better measure.

This scale, which shows statistical dispersion, was developed by an Italian sociologist (Gini 1912). It is a measure of the inequality of a distribution and now commonly used as a measure of inequality of income. A low Gini coefficient indicates a more equal distribution, with 0 corresponding to complete equality (everyone has the same income), and higher Gini coefficients indicate more unequal distribution, with 100 (or 1, on some scales) corresponding to complete inequality (one person has all the income). Because it is a measure of inequality that uses ratio analysis, it is easy to use comparatively between countries, because it ignores statistical averages such as GDP per capita. It can also be used to compare income distributions across different groups as well as between countries, and to compare income distribution over a period of time. Debraj (1998: 188) points to four particularly useful characteristics of the index: it is anonymous, it has an independent scale that is not distorted by the size of the country's economy, or the size of the population, and that its value will reflect the transferral of income from the richer to the poorer. On the other hand, countries might have identical Gini coefficients, but vary greatly in actual wealth. The coefficient doesn't take account of causes of inequity, such as structural barriers (social class, for example), and focuses on income, rather than wealth. In other words, it is a measure of the dispersal income, rather than of equality.

Table 2.1: PISA results (2009) for selected European states, with GPD per person (2010)

Country	Mathematics		Sciences		Reading		GDP	
	rank	score	Rank	score	rank	score	rank	score
Austria	13	496	18=	494	24	470	7	44,987
Belgium	4	515	10	507	3	506	9	42,630
Czech Rep	16	493	13	500	22	478	19	18,288
Denmark	8	503	14	499	13	495	3	56,147
Estonia	6	512	2	528	5=	501	21	14,836
Finland	1	541	1	554	1	536	8	44,489
France	11	497	15	498	1=	496	10	41,019
Germany	5	513	4	520	9=	497	11	40,631
Greece	24	466	23	470	19=	483	16	27,302
Hungary	18	490	11	503	14=	494	22	12,879
Iceland	7	507	16	496	7=	500	12	39,026
Ireland	19=	487	9	508	11=	496	6	45,689
Italy	22=	482	21=	488	17	486	14	34,059
Latvia	22=	482	18=	494	18	484	24	10,695
Netherlands	3	526	3	522	2	508	5	47,172
Norway	10	498	12	500	4	503	1	84,444
Poland	14	495	8	508	7=	500	23	12,300
Portugal	19=	487	20	493	16	489	18	21,559
Slovakia	12	497	7	490	23	477	20	16,104
Slovenia	9	501	21=	512	19=	483	17	23,706
Spain	21	484	17	488	21	481	15	30,639
Sweden	15	494	5	495	9=	497	4	48,875
Switzerland	2	534	6	517	5=	501	2	67,246
United Kingdom	17	492	18=	514	14=	494	13	36,120

Rankings are within the 24 selected countries, not global rankings
Sources: OECD (2009), IMF (2010)

Table 2.2: Gini coefficients for selected European countries, 2008, ordered from most equal to least equal

Country	Gini	Country	Gini	Country	Gini
Denmark	24.7	Croatia	29.0	Greece	34.3
Sweden	25.0	Austria	29.1	Ireland	34.3
Czech Republic	25.4	Bulgaria	29.2	Poland	34.5
Norway	25.8	Belarus	29.7	Spain	34.7
Slovakia	25.8	Netherlands	30.9	Estonia	35.8
Bosnia and Herzegovina	26.2	Romania	31.0	Italy	36.0
Finland	26.9	Albania	31.1	Lithuania	36.0
Hungary	26.9	Turkey	32.6	United Kingdom	36.0
Ukraine	28.1	France	32.7	Latvia	37.7
Germany	28.3	Belgium	33.0	Portugal	38.5
Slovenia	28.4	Switzerland	33.7	Macedonia	39.0

Source: Inequality in income or expenditure / Gini index, *Human Development Report 2007/08*, UNDP, accessed on February 3, 2008

The Gini ratings usefully show nearly all European states as having relatively low values: in a set of 127 ratings, Portugal, with a rating of 38.5, is 57th most equal and the most unequal European country of any size (Table 2.2). By contrast, most other major economies have more unequal income distributions: India 36.8; Russia 39.9; the USA 40.8; China 46.9 and Brazil 57.0. In comparison, Japan stands out with a much higher level of equality as demonstrated by the Gini coefficient of 24.9.

Individual and group inequities in education and wealth

The differences between scores of educational attainment and between wealth are also reflected at the individual level. Whatever the merits and demerits of IQ tests, the range of values found in the population is such that very few individuals have an IQ more than twice as great as the lowest scoring individuals. Yet inequalities in wealth are, in all countries, much greater than this.

The most detailed recent study of the effects of unequal distributions of wealth was that of Wilson and Pickett (2009). In *The Spirit Level*, they examine differences in the Gini coefficient range of income in the fifty most affluent countries, and relate this to data on the incidence of such factors as life expectancy, mental illness, addition, obesity, homicides, teenage pregnancy, imprisonment rates – and low educational performance. Taking each of these, they show close correlations between each 'social issue' and the level of difference between the richest and the poorest in each country. Note that they are only comparing the most affluent countries: they are not arguing that countries with very high levels of general poverty do not score badly on these indices. But once countries achieve an average level of GDP per head of about $15,000, further increases in average levels of wealth have very little effect on factors such as life expectancy. What does influence this in these richer countries is the distribution of wealth within the country: in countries that are most unequal, then average life expectancy is lower than in countries in which wealth is more evenly spread. This is not simply an effect of the poorer people in each of these countries: the richest individuals in the most unequal societies live less long than the richest people in the more equal societies.

The findings of Wilkinson and Pickett have been criticised, however. Besides a number of political criticisms (for example, from the Taxpayers Alliance (Sanandaji, Malm and Sanandaji 2010), there were academic criticisms. For example, Goldthorpe argued that income inequities were stressed too greatly in comparison to other potential inequities, in wealth and power, for example. Social class, he argued, was not taken properly into account, and he was critical of their 'account of the psychosocial generation of the contextual effects of inequality on health or the rival neo-materialist account' (Goldthorpe 2010).

Wade (2005) argues that inequality will have different effects in countries where inequity in power and wealth are held to be the norm, where negative effects might be less, while in the more prosperous democracies that encourage the norms of equity, and where the dominant norm is to argue for equality, then the sense of relative deprivation may be stronger (31). But Wade is here arguing across much greater disparities in wealth than are Wilkinson and Pickett, who specifically confine their argument to the more prosperous countries, where the mean GDP is over about $15,000.

In the education area, they provide graphs showing the relationship between income distribution and attainment in mathematics and literacy. Figure 2.3 shows this data in the European context.

Figure 2. 3: Mathematics and Literacy scores of 15 year olds in selected European countries

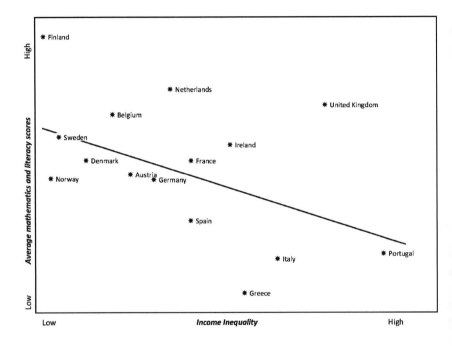

Source: based on Wilkinson and Pickett 2009: figure 8.1, p 106

Why, they ask,

> when all developed societies are committed to education and equality of opportunity (at least in theory), do disadvantaged children do less well at school, and miss out on the myriad benefits of education, however good the school system? ... Some societies come a lot closer to achieving equality ... than others (Wilkinson and Pickett 2009: 105)

They also examined the relationship between the proportion of students dropping out of high school in each state in the United States, against the Gini coefficient for each State (Figure 2.4).

Figure 2.4: Drop out from high school and income inequality in US states

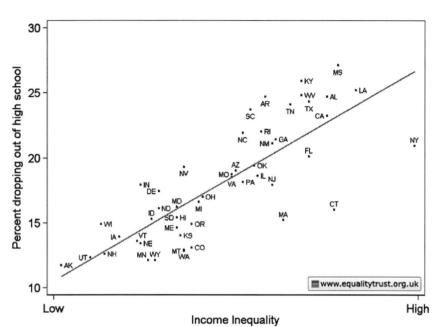

Source: Wilkinson and Pickett 2009: figure 8.3, p 107; at the Equality Trust portal
http://www.equalitytrust.org.uk/images/education.gif accessed 19 July 2011

They then compare data on literacy scores and parents' educational level
in countries with different inequalities of income, drawing on the work of
Willms (1999). Comparing the adult literacy scores (from the International
Adult Literacy Survey) with their parents' level of education, they point to
the well-established correlation between parental education and their
children's adult literacy. But the effects are different in different countries.
In the UK and the USA, where there is a high Gini coefficient of
inequality, those with parents who have a low level of education have
lower literacy scores than those with a similar parental background in
Belgium and Finland, which have lower inequality scores. Yet in all four
countries, the literacy levels for those with parents who have a high level
of education are very similar (Table 2.5). 'It looks as if the achievement of
higher national standards of educational performance may actually depend
on reducing the social gradient in educational achievement in each
country' (108).

Table 2.5: Literacy scores and parental levels of education, Finland, Belgium, UK and USA

Country	Gini Coefficient	Literacy score (parents < than middle school education)	Literacy score (parents college or higher education)	difference between two levels
Finland	26.9	253	322	67
Belgium	33.0	263	317	54
UK	36.0	244	315	71
USA	40.8	230	311	81
range		*23*	*11*	

Source: data in Wilkinson and Pickett 2009: 109

This evidence suggests that differences in the educational performances of individuals are affected by the overall level of inequities in the particular society in which the individuals live. Our major concern in this book, however, is with differences between the educational performances of groups, and how this perpetuates inequities and injustices. Performance is critical: the liberal claim that equality of opportunity is sufficient is itself and insufficient argument. The pernicious effects of inequality result from outcomes, not simply opportunities. Opportunity alone cannot overcome the radical structural inequalities that exist. Wade puts it succinctly:

> the liberal argument about globalization as the driver of benign trends in poverty and inequality is open to challenge … the seismic shift toward free market policies in the world at large over the past twenty-five years has not improved economic growth, has not reduced the number of people living on less than PPP$2 a day … and, by plausible measures of income inequality, has not made either world income distribution or national income distributions more equal. (Wade 2005: 33-34)

The moves towards the marketisation of education (eg Ball 2003) in most European states has led to schooling being seen as a commodity that leads to the achievement of better-paid employment. Education is part of the grading system that gives credentials that can be used to obtain work (or access to higher education for the same ends). This changes the nature of education. From being something that has at least the potential to be based on criteria – being able to do something, being able to understand something – the market inevitably requires that educational outputs becomes normatively-referenced. Whereas an examination to test the ability to drive a car is something that almost everyone can potentially achieve, a school or college examination necessarily has become something that requires some to fail.

It is in the interest of those who can give their children the cultural capital to succeed in the school system to ensure that other children fail. Unlike a driving test, or being able to swim, or access to health care – where it does not matter if others succeed or fail – educational examinations and qualifications only 'work' for the offspring of dominant and powerful groups if the children of less powerful groups are marked as failures. The marketised educational system requires teachers and educationalists not simply to assess and grade, but to categorise successes and failures, because only such a process can divide and segregate. Education becomes a competitive enterprise, setting student against student, school against school, nation against nation, creating a barrage of rhetoric that creates and sustains inequalities, and a set of discourses that are used to explain and justify inequities and group successes and failures. In the next chapter we examine some of the arguments that have been used to justify educational inequalities. Excuses and evasions are then discussed in more detail in the fourth chapter while discourse as part of the construction of inequality is re-examined from another perspective in chapter five.

CHAPTER THREE

OUTCOMES, OPPORTUNITIES AND EXPLANATIONS

This chapter focuses on policy and research assumptions and explanations that have been used over the past twenty to thirty years to justify and sustain approaches to educational underachievement by different social groups. We have already explained that it is underachievement by social groups, rather than underachievement by individuals, that is the focus of our study. The last thirty years have been characterised by a growing awareness of differences in group attainment, and how these differences are seen between groups. This has in turn stimulated policy drives to try and raise the attainment of underachieving groups, thus lowering the difference between higher and lower achieving groups. However, there are a variety of explanations about why there are inter-group differences in attainment, and these affect the choice and nature of the policies adopted. There are also a number of different rationales or justifications advanced for attempting to minimise inter-group differences and raise attainment: these too affect the choice of policies.

We begin with an analysis of these different explanations, and then consider the range of social groups that have been described as underachieving. Following this, we examine how these groups are constructed and identified, and how there might be multiple aspects in underachievement. The identification of group categories, and of explanations for under-attainment, are, of course, social constructions, and this will also be considered (this is also re-visited in chapter five). In particular, it raises questions about the consequences of labelling particular groups as underachieving, and the focus on policies that seek to 'remedy' this, and the creation of low expectations, an issue that will be returned to in more detail in chapters four and five. This chapter concludes with a brief examination of some of the possible markers that might be used to establish the existence, types and levels of educational inequity.

Explanations offered for the persistence of educational inequalities

There are a variety of current explanations of why educational disadvantage persists, at both societal and governmental level. Pervading most of these is the general discourse of meritocracy, which has developed over recent decades. This is the argument that any system that seeks efficiency should ensure that 'the best' can 'rise' to the top. Appointments are made, and responsibilities given to those individuals who can best demonstrate their intelligence and ability, and these factors are very often assessed by educational performance. A high level of educational performance gives access to positions and experience that then allows the individual to accumulate more evidence of intelligence and ability, and denies (or at least hinders access) such experience to those with lesser levels of performance. This is a particularly insidious argument: it implies that those who do not succeed – even entire groups of people – are themselves responsible for any disadvantages they suffer. It discounts institutional and structural impediments to success, and ignores the fact that those who do 'succeed' in a meritocracy take steps to ensure that their children become embedded in structures that will ensure that they succeed regardless of 'merit'. Diamond and Giddens (2005) observed that 'pure meritocracy is incoherent because, without redistribution, one generation's successful individuals would become the next generation's embedded caste, hoarding the wealth they had accumulated'.

It is often forgotten that the term meritocracy was originally conceived and used as a satirical argument against mixing conceptions of equality with notions of merit (in a novel, *The Rise of the Meritocracy* (Young 1958). Michael Young was a sociologist and social entrepreneur, highly influential in the UK for all the second half of the twentieth century: the novel mockingly points to how an elite selected on merit would inevitably seek to ensure, through arrogance and complacency, that the privileged positions they rose to would be passed on to their offspring, even though they might well be less talented. His argument was that any attempt to give special status of an elite as being particularly important to society – a 'creative minority' or a 'restless elite', as he put it, would produce a much larger majority of the disempowered: 'Every selection of one is the rejection of man' (Young 1958: 15).

Writing just before his death in 2002, Young observed wryly on how his satire had been misunderstood and misused:

It is good sense to appoint individual people to jobs on their merit. It is the opposite when those who are judged to have merit of a particular kind harden into a new social class without room in it for others. Ability of a conventional kind, which used to be distributed between the classes more or less at random, has become much more highly concentrated by the engine of education. A social revolution has been accomplished by harnessing schools and universities to the task of sieving people according to education's narrow band of values. With an amazing battery of certificates and degrees at its disposal, education has put its seal of approval on a minority, and its seal of disapproval on the many who fail to shine from the time they are relegated to the bottom streams at the age of seven or before. The new class has the means at hand, and largely under its control, by which it reproduces itself.

... I expected that the poor and the disadvantaged would be done down, and in fact they have been. If branded at school they are more vulnerable for later unemployment. They can easily become demoralised by being looked down on so woundingly by people who have done well for themselves.

In the new social environment, the rich and the powerful have been doing mighty well for themselves. ... The newcomers can actually believe they have morality on their side. As a result, general inequality has been becoming more grievous with every year that passes, and without a bleat from the leaders of the party who once spoke up so trenchantly and characteristically for greater equality. (Young 2001)

The meritocratic fallacy pervades much of the justification for educational underachievement. It is predicated on the assumption that the principal purpose of an educational system is to filter and grade individual's attainment, rather than to equip them with the abilities, skills and understanding to become fulfilled members of society. The system, as Young eloquently puts it, is designed to create failures: this makes inequality, with all its social consequences (Wilkinson and Pickett 2009), inevitable. Even more alarming is that the practice of meritocracy has, in many countries, created whole social groups that 'fail', and this institutionalises and codifies underachievement, offering reassuring rationalisations for social differences and justifying discriminatory practices against social groups, be they social classes, ethnicities, the disabled or any other minority.

At any one time one can detect a mixture of some or all of a number of explanations of why disadvantage may be evident, each bringing with it implicit and explicit implications for policies that might redress the situation. They represent a wide variety of debates, from 'commonsense' explanations found in popular media discourse to more elaborated arguments and explanations. The assumptions of meritocracy seem to pervade them all. Some are quite historic and outdated, but nevertheless are still employed today, and are not always challenged. All of the following explanations have been offered over the past two or three decades.

Pathological explanations

There are still suggestions that any inequality is largely the consequence of individual characteristics or behaviour, or possibly group characteristics. For example, some people have taken the view that intelligence is largely genetically determined, and that therefore no amount of education, or additional targeted educational resources is likely to make a difference in achieved performance. In the United States context, Herrnstein and Murray (1994) and Murray (1984) claim that Afro-Americans inevitably achieve less intellectually and economically than white Americans, for pathological reasons – a nexus of genetic and cultural endowment that makes them dysfunctional. Many writers have powerfully contested this, for example Spicker (2006) and Kärfve (2000) and Apple (2001). Apple refers to this as 'the popularisation of what is clearly a form of social Darwinist thinking, as the recent popularity of *The Bell Curve* (Herrnstein and Murray 1994) in the USA and elsewhere so obviously and distressingly indicates' (2001: 410-11).

The genetic argument is now becoming discredited, as the recent advances in understanding the limitations of genetic inheritance show that humans simply have too few genes to account for the range of different abilities that the human species display (Richardson and Boyd 2005). With only 25,000 genes, Craig Venter, leader of the Human Genome Project, concluded 'We simply do not have enough genes for this idea of biological determinism to be right. The wonderful diversity of the human species is not hard-wired in our genetic code. Our environments are critical' (quoted by Ho 2001). Edmund Sonuga-Barke, a leading specialist in attention-deficit hyperactivity syndrome and editor of the *Journal of Child Psychology and Psychiatry* observed that in terms of behaviour and attainment 'serious science is now more than ever focused on the power of the environment - all but the most dogged of genetic determinists have revised their view of the primacy of genetic factors' (2010: 113).

Transmitted deprivation

Partly related to the previous explanation, another argument made by some is that the poor educational attainment of individuals or groups can be attributed to their upbringing. The anthropologist Oscar Lewis (1963) suggested that 'the poor' often formed an autonomous subculture that socialised its children with reinforced attitudes and behaviours that trapped them in the underclass.

> The people in the culture of poverty have a strong feeling of marginality, of helplessness, of dependency, of not belonging. They are like aliens in their own country, convinced that the existing institutions do not serve their interests and needs. Along with this feeling of powerlessness is a widespread feeling of inferiority, of personal unworthiness. (Lewis 1963: 17)

The term 'cycle of deprivation' developed out of this, which stressed the importance of intergenerational continuities and was used to suggest that disadvantaged parents may have 'deficient' parenting skills, and their children therefore will also have disadvantages in terms of educational outcomes, and pass these on to their own children (Joseph 1972). This was used to make the family responsible for the lack of achievement: as Connell put it,

> the failure of access was read outward from the institutions to the families they served. Families and children became berated for a deficit for which the institutions should compensate (Connell 1994: 129)

The theory has remained popular, despite a series of empirical studies showing that it was unsound (Rutter and Madge 1976; Jeffrey 1978; Silver and Silver 1991; Berthoud 1983; Welshman 2006a, b).

> Research has demonstrated that there is substantial intergenerational continuity; that the continuities are more marked for the more severe problems than for the minor ones; but also that there are marked discontinuities; that resilience helps to explain individual differences; and that the continuities are greater looking backwards than looking forwards. Moreover much more is known now about mediating processes, both within the family (such as poor parenting), and outside the family (such as overall living conditions), and these point to a synergistic interaction between them. Thus this research points to an interplay between risk and protective processes, and between proximal and distal risk mechanisms, and is much more cautious about assigning causes to what are recognised as multifactorial disorders. (Rutter 2006: 12 -1 3)

Despite this, the explanation is still offered in some policy circles (West 2007). For example, the social heritage model, popular in some Scandinavian countries, was particularly advanced in Denmark with reference to the education of delinquent children (Jonsson 1969), as a counter to medicalised or pathological explanations related to genetics or biology. *Negativt social arv* (negative social heritage) refers to 'poor' family culture and a low social class position, with the associated negative markers these bring. There have been significant critiques of this (in Denmark by Sivertsen (2007), and in Sweden by Vinnerljung (1998). In the UK, a report by the Social Exclusion Unit (*Breaking the Cycle,* ODPM 2004) referred to an 'intergenerational cycle of deprivation', along with the 'transmission' and 'inheritance' of disadvantage (10, 28).

The explanation is also applied to whole cultural groups in poverty, so that the culture itself, as well as its families, are stigmatised as dysfunctional, transmitting inadequate behaviour from one generation to the next. For example, the Roma population across Europe are not uncommonly characterised as having dysfunctional familial patterns that 'transmit' deprivation from generation to generation (for example, in Spain see Dooly and Vallejo 2008 ; in Greece Spinthourakis, Karatzia-Stavlioti, Lempesi, and Papadimitriou,2008).

The policy implications of such an explanation would be to target resources at interventions in parenting, in order to remedy presumed 'deficits'. But Gordon *et al.* (1999) thoroughly investigated such claims, and very effectively dismissed them as not having any standing in reality. Many studies of intergenerational continuity have found that most children of disadvantaged parents are not themselves subsequently disadvantaged (see chapter five for more discussion).

Home based factors

Other analysts and commentators suggest that the principal cause of poor educational achievement is material deprivation, for example, through poor health or a lack of resources in the home (such as books) and lack of facilities (like a quiet place to do homework). The correlation between the number of books and attainment is often very striking (Evans 2004, Evans, Kelley, Sikora, Treiman 2010), but this cannot be seen as a causal factor (would giving a couple of hundred books to homes with underachieving children transform the situation?). If the family size and family environment affect the degree of stimulation a child receives, and hence affect development, then policy initiates should direct resources at the general alleviation of poverty with associated programmes to improve parental understanding of such home based factors. These factors are often used to identify non-mainstream parenting practices, often in a process of stigmatisation. Examples can be seen in some attitudes towards the Roma (see above), and in some countries Muslim home factors are similarly used to 'explain' poor educational performance. Homes where the principal language is not the national language can sometimes be similarly characterised as offering a deprived background (Muller and Beardsmore 2004; Dooly, Vallejo and Unamuno 2009). Educational policies that provide homework centres for pupils whom it is presumed will not have help or guidance at home are a response (for example, in Denmark, Undervisningsministeriet 2005).

The view that the families of working class families is somehow less educationally rich than that of middle class families developed from misunderstandings (perhaps not unwittingly) from readings of Bourdieu's notion of habitus and cultural capital (1973; see above), and Bernstein's work on restricted and elaborated codes of languages (1971, 1975): Bernstein protested vigorously at such misreading (1974). The impoverished home background explanation overlaps with the cycle of poverty analysis (see, for example, Griffin (1993). The idea that the poor have a distinct culture and attitudes has been widely critiqued: Hoyles (1977) refers to the way that studies such as Oscar Lewis's were conducted within an anthropological framework. Connell points to how such a framework is not infrequently linked with a psychological twist, and this combination could be interpreted to mean that:

> Cultural differences in the group meant psychological deficits in the individual: that is a lack of the traits necessary to succeed in school. With this twist, a wide range of research could be read as demonstrating cultural deprivation, from studies of linguistic codes to occupational expectations to achievement motivation to IQ, and so on. In the 1960s and 1970s, the cultural deficit concept became folklore amongst teachers as well as policymakers. (Connell 1994: 131; citing Interim Committee for the Australian Schools Commission 1973)

The problems with this form of analysis are many. There are individual examples of high-achieving individuals who come from materially deprived homes, so the correlation is not complete. There are many cultural factors within economically deprived families that determine the allocation of family resources (money, the use of space, and time: Coleman's 1968 study on the socio-economically deprived will be referred to later in this chapter). The lack of recognition of such diversity can lead to a discourse of deficit and of blaming parents as feckless and irresponsible (discussed further in chapter five).

The identification of programmes to 'compensate' for shortcomings in educational achievements, and their attachment to specified groups of the population, becomes a process that is used to justify and explain why a group is 'deficient'. 'The very existence of such programs now evokes the rationale of deficiency' (Connell 1994: 131). Casanova pointed to the effect on members of the groups concerned: such activities 'assaulted their social selves with labels like 'learning-disabled'' (Casanova 1990: 148; see also chapter five).

Expectations in the Classroom: School factors

A fourth current explanation is that disadvantage and inequitable outcomes arise from the failure of schools to respond to pupils' needs. Aspects of this might include low levels of resources, a limited curriculum, and low teacher expectations, all of which might be further exacerbated by streaming, the restrictive examination system (both of which can lead to lowered teacher expectations), and high teacher turnover. (We will discuss this further, from a discursive interactional perspective, in chapter five). The very well-known studies that demonstrate how low teacher expectations of particular groups leads to low performance by the group include Pygmalion in the Classroom (Rosenthal and Jacobs 1968), but can be found both much earlier (Merton 1948) and also in more recent studies (Brophy and Good 1974; Good 1987; Brophy 1998; Ferguson 1998; see also Dooly 2009 for a discourse analysis of the Pygmalion Effect). The argument here is that good schools can make a difference, and that resources should be directed at enhancing school organisation, resources, and teachers' abilities and attitudes. The classic study by Rutter and his associates (1979) suggests that schools can make significant differences. A range of educational practices identified in this study show the wide prevalence of teacher expectations of particular categories leading to underperformance – for example, among ethnic minorities (Gilborn and Youdell 2000; Francis 2007), linguistic minorities (Council of Europe 2003; Tozzi and Étienne 2008; Dooly *et al* 2009). This group of explanations will be examined in more detail in subsequent chapters.

Structural views

Structural theories relate educational disadvantage to the structure of society. These sociological and political explanations argue that class disadvantages and poverty are reflected in educational attainment because of the combination of home and school factors: low reservoirs of cultural capital, socio-economic disadvantage, and educational structures designed to maintain inequalities (such as hierarchies of school types, socially differentiated curricula, etc). Post-structural views have a relation to this set of explanations, relating to the discursive construction of inequalities. Major theorists include Bourdieu (1973; Bourdieu and Passeron 1977) and Bowles and Gintis (1976) (referred to above); Giddens has also extensively explored structuration (1984, 1991). Kluegel (1990) has referred to the way in which structural explanations can be (mis)used in explanations of racial differences in motivation and attainment, in what is often called 'blaming the victim' (see also Ryan 1976). In Sweden, there was systematic investigation into the extent to which structural discrimination and related factors affected educational attainment (Sawyer and Kamali 2006; Runfors 2006). In some countries, restructuring educational provision, particularly in the creation of 'action zones', has been a response to this analysis – for example, in Cyprus in the early 2000s (Cyprus *nd*), and in England, much earlier in the 1970s as Educational Priority Areas (CACE 1967) and again in 1998 as Educational Action Zones (UK 1998).

Poststructuralist explanations

Post-structuralist theories give central attention to the concept of discourse, as a set of practices and beliefs that produce what they pretend to describe. As Davies argued,

> … in poststructuralist theory the focus is on the way each person actively takes up the discourses through which they and others speak/write the world into existence as if it were their own. (Davies 1993: 13)

The Poststructuralist position would argue that the foregoing accounts are rationales for inequity have all been constructed around the wrong targets, and are based on assumptions and power discourses that need to be analysed further, especially theorists working in the field of Critical Discourse Analysis (cf. Fowler 1991; Fowler, Hodge, Kress, and Trew 1979; Atkinson and Heritage 1984; Fairclough 1989, 1995, 2001; Ng and Bradac 1993; Gee 1996, 2005; McKenna 2004).

In practice, this means that groups or individuals positioned as, for example, under-achieving in the dominant educational discourse of, for example, ethnicity or gender, may also challenge such positionings (cf. Christie 2002; Mehta and Ninnes 2003; Rogers 2004). So, while recognising the influence of ethnicity, gender, etc., the focus of post-structuralism is on the agency and the fluidity of the self. Deconstructing the ways in which the earlier 'explanations' of inequity have been presented shows that they have all taken for granted that educational attainment is an objective and measurable reality, and that there is a spectrum of attainment, on which identifiable groups can be positioned. Poststructuralists would argue that these processes of categorisation, naming and measuring are themselves the product of a particular social hegemony.

Poststructuralist theories also argue that while gender, social class, ethnicity, etc. are usually categorised as dual, oppositional and fixed, they are fluid and multiple aspects of the self. In educational theory, the study of nursery school boys' interaction with a woman teacher by Walkerdine (1998) represents an infamous illustration of individuals' agency and of the fluidity and multiplicity of the self, as the nursery boys contest their position as 'dominated' in the pupil-teacher interaction to position their teacher as 'dominated' (and, thus, themselves as 'dominant').

Such a position may be useful to challenge the essentialist orthodoxies that pervade much policy analysis in this area. But it must also be recognised that policy creation and implementation does not happen in a social vacuum: it must necessarily take place within the various discourses of a society (though recognising that there are a variety of competing discourses does, to an extent, in itself recognise the poststructuralist position). And it must also be recognised that policy and implementation are necessarily urgent and immediate: schools have to open tomorrow, and teachers have to prepare for this tonight. Time to undertake the analysis of discourses is a luxury that the professional policy community and educational practice community must address alongside daily activity, not in advance of it. This focus on the interaction and interplay between different discourses (individual and collective) and their role in the social construction of power is examined in more detail in chapter five.

These various explanations offer radically different interpretations – even different belief systems – about why various groups may have different levels of educational performance. As has already been indicated, groups of educational policies have developed that are linked (explicitly or implicitly) to one or other of these explanations. This means that the programmes are, understandably, based on a set of beliefs about why the 'problem' has come about. It should be already clear that many of these explanations are not just mutually exclusive, but based on opposing beliefs about the causes of inequality between groups. But this is not the only reason why policies are so radically diverse. In chapter two we reviewed the different conceptions of why educational inequalities were (or were not) an issue that might be considered important. Different motivations for action – based either on instrumentalism or on rights – will also lead to differences in policies. A third dimension is found in the ways in which groups are indentified as being subject to educational inequalities, and it is to this we now turn.

What kinds of groups are disadvantaged, and why?

In the opening chapter we explained that our concern would be with inequities between social groups, rather than between individuals. Individuals will differ in their interests, abilities, motivations and successes: there is an inevitable variety in this. The rules of exclusion can be based either on group membership, or on individual characteristics (Brown and Compton 1994). Such a distinction in terms of rights and inequity dates back to the writings about individual rights by Rousseau (1762/1968), and about group rights by Wollstonecraft (1792/2009). Contemporary European policy directives emphasise that group inequities exist, particularly in terms of attainment and economic integration (European Commission 1993; 1994, 2007).

But why do groups differ in these characteristics of attainment? Groups are collections of individuals, so group differences are the sum of individual variations. But does membership of group mean that the general level of such characteristics should be different for the average of the overall population? We suggested that there should be a general presumption that all groups might be expected to perform and behave at similar levels in educational settings. Our starting point should be that if a particular group, as a whole, has a lower attainment than that of the total population as a whole, then we should assume that there is something in the way the educational policies and/or practices of that society have operated to discriminate against the group. As we noted earlier, this does not necessarily mean that there has to be overt, or intended, discrimination. It is quite possible – indeed, not uncommon – for educational institutions to have very specific policies that explicitly aim at the elimination of inequities, and to provide equal opportunities and equal outcomes, and still to operate in such a way that they discriminate negatively in terms of group outcomes. There will also be instances when policies and practices are more intentionally designed to discriminate; and others where positive educational policies coexist with prejudicial attitudes and behave in broader society, and compete and conflict with these.

So what are the groups that we suggest suffer inequalities? Which groups appear to be disadvantaged, and why? Competition between groups is at least a partial explanation: more powerful groups can maintain their hegemony, and rationalise their advantage, ascribing explanations for underachievement on less powerful groups. As Weber observed,

> Usually one group of competitors take on some externally identifiable characteristic of another group of (actual or potential) competitors – race, language, religion, local or social origin, descent, resident, etc. – as a pretext for attempting their exclusion. It does not matter which characteristic is chosen in the individual case: whatever suggests itself is most easily seized upon (Weber 1968: 242)

There are also hierarchies inherent in individualism and individual property rights, that allows what Ball, Bowe and Gewirtz (1994: 24) call a 'thin morality' based on the competitive individualism of the market, but group differentiation and hierarchies are different, though often correlated to individual hierarchies.

We will suggest a number of parameters that may be used to help in the identification of a potentially disadvantaged group. But we should begin by pointing out that these groups are defined heuristically, socially constructed because they seem to be relevant at the time. This is not a criticism of this process of group identification – the fact that their definition is contingent indicates a social awareness that the category potentially has some relevance for policy and practice. But such groupings are necessarily temporary: they will change and transmogrify as the context and setting change. Nor are these groups hermetically sealed from each other – they are not exclusive categories, but intersect with other categorisations. Many individuals and sub-sets will be doubly or trebly disadvantaged by their membership of two or three categories (or more).

Such fluid definitions upset some analysts. Because they are not clear cut and absolute, we must necessarily be imprecise about who is a member of the group. If an individual elects to categorise themselves as member of a particular group, we may have little choice but to accept this definition. To give a concrete example, in some countries individuals define their own ethnicity: it is argued that this is an element of their personal identity, and only they are qualified to declare their identity, or this aspect of it. Others, for example, may wish to declare their own gender orientation – which may differ from their biological sex. It can be argued that it is not for an outsider, another person (least of all for the state) to assign individuals to an ethnicity or a gender orientation, based on some 'objective' criterion. But others object to this. Some do so on the grounds that there can be criteria that assign people to a particular ethnic category – for example, their ancestry. *Jus sanguinis* allows nationality to those descended from a defined group. But problems arise when an individual has mixed ethnic origins. *Jus solis* is more precise, and less open to challenge. Both become fairly meaningless in the context of globalisation – there are far many more people of mixed descent; and family movements can mean that, under *jus solis*, different members of the same family can have different status imposed on them.

Another criticism of such a policy is that self-identification encourages social fragmentation and individuals 'playing the ethnic card' (eg Sunier 2004: 239-40, Mannitz 2004: 319a). It can further be argued that these groups are defined as socially excluded entirely in terms of the market economy, in a way that excludes other aspects of social life, and possibly thus detracting from other social inequalities (Levitas 1996). The identification of disadvantaged groups may also allow parents to disengage from community schools and to maintain educational exclusivity (Apple 2001: 418).

We argue here for a more pragmatic approach that allows groups to be identified and analysed in response to perceptions of inequality and difference. The purpose of defining groups and analysing their educational attainments should, we argue, be related to and based on policies and practices. Defining a group (albeit imperfectly, pragmatically, by self-identification) allows policy makers to analyse the particular educational performance of members of the group. This in turn allows analysing the possible causes of underperformance, and the targeting of support measures that may address this – the identification of the group (and its size, and location, allows this). Finally, it allows the tracking of changes in performance over time, to monitor the effectiveness (or not) of the targeted measures (see, for example, the changes in attainments shown by Bangladeshi-origin children in the UK (Ofsted 2004; Strand *et al.*).

We seek to comment on analyses of a range of different types of educational disadvantage, because different social groups suffer disproportionately from different kinds of social disadvantage. We suggest that while it is important that policies focus on *specific* requirements, and are implemented and monitored to address those needs, we also need to look at the various groups that suffer educational disadvantage. The widely-used category of socio-economic disadvantage has many related aspects. The conception of social capital, and exclusion from this relates to a range of potential categories: it is likely to correlate and intersect with minority ethnic and indigenous status, with minority language status, and with disability. Similarly, there are significant gender differences in income in most European states, thus intersecting gender with economic status. (The difficulties of 'pinpointing' single factors for inequality, due to the myriad of social interactions that influence outcomes, is discussed from the perspective of 'Complexity Theory' further on in this book.)

The outcomes of the educational process can demonstrate inequality in various ways, differently illustrating how forms of disadvantage can become institutionally entrenched. For example, selecting different educational outcomes as measures can demonstrate how different groups are disadvantaged: leaving formal education at an early age, for example, is a particular outcome characteristic of pupils from economically disadvantaged groups, while low educational attainment, although linked to this, may also be a characteristic particular to certain ethnic minority groups. But the disadvantage suffered by young women as a result of educational processes are not necessarily because of their length of education or their levels of achievement (in several countries these are better than males), but in the way that the curriculum institutionalises gendered identities and opportunities.

The issues of how and why various categories are identified and named (and are thus socially constructed) have consequences in terms of how people have a sense of themselves. It can be seen as allowing the construction of practice *vis a vis* educational participation in ways that reify the category. As well as the potential to empower a community, there is also the possibility of shifting responsibility onto the community or the individuals in the community to solve the problems for themselves: the neo-liberal offer of a 'choice' can shift the onus for change to a group who may not be in any sense responsible for, or able to address, wider structural and attitudinal causes (Dovemark 2004; Hartsmar 2008: 5, 27). Identifying a new category makes possible new practices and performances for those who have been labelled (see, for example, Kärfve 2000, and Hartsmar 2008: 22). Identification of an 'at risk' category inevitably has social consequences. There are also issues concerning different categorisation practices and terminology in different countries (for example, in special educational needs in Belgium (Lambrechts, Geurts and Verkest 2008) and in minority ethnic groups in the Netherlands (Geurts and Lambrechts 2008). It is important to recognise that intersectionality is a critical factor in understanding the multiple identities and categories that arise (Moreau 2008: 157-8; Ross 2008: 91-104). Thus, for example, in Denmark coming from an immigrant background is strongly correlated to poverty (Dahl 2005) and educational disadvantage is strongly related to both a poor social economic background and to poor levels of use of Danish (Christensen and Sloth 2005). In Sweden, Behtoui (2006) showed the intersection between ethnic background and social background, the former being used in popular discourse to discount the effect of poor living conditions: social class acquires an ethnic face (see also Moldenhawer 2001).

Thus many groups will suffer educational disadvantage through multiple aspects – for example, being both poor, members of an ethnic and religious minority, and speaking a different language to that of the majority of the population. Each of these attributes may contribute to the overall disadvantage in a different manner, and it is useful, for analytic purposes, to identify how marginalisation and disadvantage are identified and created through different categories.

A further aspect of this has been the development of newly recognised categories, for example in disabilities: Leathwood (2008) notes the issues in accurately categorising some of these, as many of them are self-declared and socially constructed (also Kärvfe 2000). In the UK again, minority ethnic categories are being subdivided as differences in educational attainment are detected: the category 'Black African' (itself distinguished from 'Black Caribbean' and 'Black Other') is now sometimes divided, in the context of education, into extended codes to differentiate differently achieving groups.

It is also important to recognise that neither minority status nor difference –as categories– in themselves necessarily imply disadvantage, or inequality. There are many examples of different groups that are not educationally disadvantaged, and this study is concerned only with groups that are educationally disadvantaged. It is acknowledged upfront that the potential categories that we describe below will have examples within them of groups and sub-groups that are fully incorporated into the educational mainstream, and achieve a distribution of achievement and outcome that are the same as that of the rest of the population.

Socio-economic disadvantage

Economic disadvantage is a major (and perhaps a significantly underlying) characteristic of educational disadvantage. Coleman suggested (1966, 1968) that socio-economic status is significantly more important in determining educational outcomes than differences in school resources. Poverty has been described as being a comparative and normative concept, and not as an absolute term (Townsend 1979): this realisation put the economic changes of the post-war thirty years (*les Trente Glorieuses*) into a new context of social inequalities. Along these lines of relativity, family poverty has been shown to be a significant marker of educational underachievement, however, as Connell (1994) stresses, it is only a partial explanation, and one that may, moreover, lead to compensatory programmes that reinforce inequalities. Apple (2001) points to

> [t]he rise in importance of cultural capital infiltrates all institutions in such a way that there is a relative movement away from the *direct* reproduction of class privilege (where power is transmitted largely within families through economic property) to *school mediated* forms of class privilege. Here, 'the bequeathal of privilege is simultaneously effectuated and transfigured by the intercession of educational institutions' (Wacquant, 1996, p. xiii). This is *not* a conspiracy; it is not 'conscious' in the ways we normally use that concept. Rather it is the result of a long chain of relatively autonomous connections between differentially accumulated economic, social, and cultural capital operating at the level of daily events as we make our respective ways in the world, including as we saw in the world of school choice. (2001: 420)

These processes allow the state to shift the blame for the inequalities in opportunities and outcomes - that it claims it intends to mitigate and reduce – from its own policies to the practices of the students, parents and the schools (Apple 2001: 416).

Social class thus remains a significant variable in the analysis of inequalities in the work of many educational analysts (Thrupp 1995;

Mickelwright 2003; Reay 2006). However, economic disadvantage alone does not explain all social disadvantages, and other categories must also be employed to explain the institutionalisation of disadvantage and discrimination.

Minority ethnic disadvantage

This is often linked to other aspects of disadvantage, for example, that experienced by people from some minority ethnic communities, whether settlers, refugees or asylum seekers, who suffer also from racism. Some countries, however, refuse to collect data on minority ethnic status, noting both that its self-definitional nature may lead to lack of consistency, and suggesting that identifying ethnic groups is in itself racist, and in the belief that identifying minorities counters an inclusive republican definition of inclusive citizenship. Other countries hold that racism can only be challenged by identifying these groups, and then targeting provision and monitoring achievement. Some countries identify ethnic minorities that have settled in the country for several generations as 'immigrant', even though they may no longer have meaningful associations with the country of origin of their grandparents, while other countries use the term 'migrant' only to include the individuals who have migrated. These categories can therefore, in some countries, become blurred with indigenous minorities. Longstanding indigenous minorities, of which the Roma are but one example, are not infrequently the victims of xenophobia and of educational disadvantage (see, for example, Pinnock 2001). However, the definition of this group shows marked variations between different countries, and sometimes minorities that have lived in the territory for several hundred years are still not considered 'indigenous'. In some countries (for example, the Czech Republic, the Netherlands, Spain) terms borrowed from geology to differentiate 'original' rocks from those that have been deposited by sedimentary action ('autochthonous' and 'allocthonous') have been used to justify differentiating groups that have no links with any other territory.

Disability as disadvantage

People with disabilities are another group for whom educational attainment data suggests that some sub-groups may be disadvantaged. The term disability has been recognised in recent years to encompass a much greater range than impaired physical abilities.

Gender, sexuality and disadvantage

Gender is an area in which there is a range of often deeply-ingrained attitudes that lead to different social expectations of roles, and hence to discriminatory and disadvantaging practices in areas of social reproduction such as education (Rees 1998: 15). Stereotypical behaviours can lead to gendered practices in educational provision and expectation. While in many cases, women and girls achieve comparatively better educational standards than men and boys, they nevertheless find that subject choices can be constrained by assumptions about future roles, and that employment prospects are inhibited. Under this broad heading, we would also refer to educationally discriminatory behaviour and disadvantage towards individual's sexual orientation, particularly as this may affect lesbians, gays, bisexuals and transgendered individuals (Leathwood *et al.* 2008, Council of Europe 2011). Many educational policies construct social attitudes that condone gender discrimination.

Linguistic minorities and disadvantage

There are many examples of equating a dominant language as *the* language of a particular country. This may lead to social practices that marginalise and discriminate against linguistic minorities. Many of these are long-standing minority languages in the country that are widely spoken in particular regions, but may not have official recognition. Others are world languages that have more recently established themselves within particular communities who have migrated to and settled in Europe. Educational practices that discriminate against languages other than the mainstream are particularly damaging to pupils whose home language is different. There is much evidence that children need to be supported in the development of their home language in order to achieve future linguistic competence, and that such support greatly sustains the development of bilingualism and multilingualism. Conversely, attempts to suppress or ignore the home language, or to forbid its use in schools or in public places, undermine both individual development and social cohesion. We also note with concern hierarchical attitudes towards different languages, privileging national languages over regional, and regional languages over world languages (Dooly *et al* 2009). This list is not to suggest that there are necessarily deliberate policies of discrimination in these areas, but that, even unwittingly, the effects of existing policies create, sustain and may even accentuate the degree of disadvantage. Nor are these necessarily the only groups who may suffer educational disadvantage.

European Union institutions are variously expressing concerns about inequalities in education. The availability of such data from comparative surveys such as the Programme for International Student Assessment (PISA) and Trends in International Mathematics and Science Study (TIMSS) makes it possible to identify particular areas of concern. For example, in the Commission's Green Paper *Migration and mobility: challenges and opportunities for EU education systems* (European Commission 2007) PISA data was used in the following two figures (Figure 3.1, Figure 3.2).

These figures clearly identify differential attainment between migrant and non-migrant young people, and differences between each county's ability to respond to these. The commissioning of the EPASI analysis, to which we refer in the opening chapter, and on which some of this study is based, was in part a response of the Commission to this kind of data.

Studies such as PISA, organised by the OECD, thus provide valuable comparative data about educational outcomes, in a significant (though limited) number of areas (see, for example, European Commission 2004; Haar *et al* 2005; Stanat *et al* 2006; Heckmann 2008). This is not contradictory to our argument in chapter two that the use of standardised, national testing can be a tool for promotion of Neo-Liberal ideals. We propose here that such tests must be used carefully and with other comparative data to help promote equal outcomes in education for all groups.

Figure 3.1 - Differences in student performance in reading, by immigrant status and country (Performance on the reading scale – mean score)

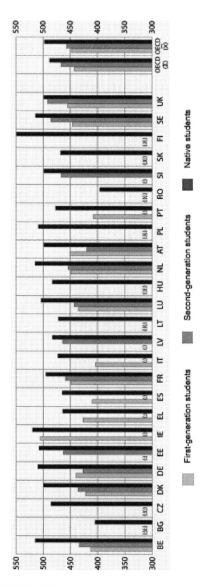

Data source: OECD PISA 200

Figure 3.2 - Share of early school leavers by nationality, 2005 (Percentage of the population aged 18-24 with only lower-secondary education and not in education or training, by nationality, 2005)

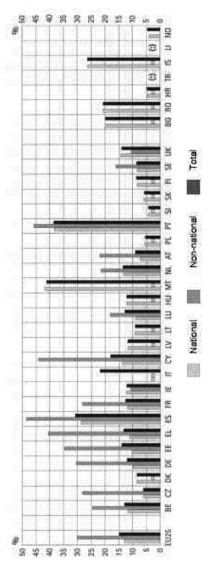

Data source: Eurostat (Labour Force Survey), 200 (Originally Figures 3 and 5, taken from European Commission (2007) pp 6 -7)

Markers for inequalities

How is it possible to tell whether a particular group is suffering from some form of educational inequality? It might be suggested that one should examine the processes of education to identify precisely differences in treatment and approach. But this would be extraordinarily difficult to do in a systematic comparative study. Processes may be examined through qualitative case studies, but the expense and time to generate sufficient data to compare processes in a way that might be generalised across countries would be immense. Policy analysis and the evaluation of outcomes are both more promising approaches, though will not necessarily identify gaps between policy intentions and implementation, or the teaching and learning practices that create particular outcomes.

An interesting approach to comparative policy analysis is demonstrated by the Migration Integration Policy Index (MIPEX) (Huddleston, Niessen, Chaoimh and White 2011). This sought to compare different countries' educational policies towards migrants and their children. Policy indicators were derived from various international conventions and statements of rights (whether finally ratified or not), from bodies such as the United Nations, UNESCO, the International Labour Organisation and the OECD, or European statements or directives from, for example, the Council of Europe or the European Commission. Indicators of policy compliance were created for each of these, and different countries' policies then measured against each of 24 such indicators (for a full description, see Ross 2011).

Similarly, we also suggest that countries – and the European Commission - need to use indicators that indicate inequalities of outcome. The emphasis must be on educational *outcomes*, rather than on educational *opportunities*, and should be significant and deliberate. We need evidence of differences between the achievement or performance of a group when compared to the prevailing national norm. This is not always straightforward, or indeed possible, because of the very wide variety of ways in which data is collected in different countries, and, as has been noted above, the different categories and conceptualisations of difference that are found between countries. The prime analysis has to be conducted at the national level, where comparison can be made between a particular group and the national norm. Some countries provide detailed analysis of the educational attainment of some disadvantaged groups (for a detailed example, see Department for Education and Skills 2006), but in no country did we find reports on all these areas of potential inequality.

The following seven suggested markers of outcomes are indicative, rather than prescriptive. If the outcomes of different groups for a particular marker are significantly different, then there would be a prima fascia case of educational inequity towards the group. If the differences occurred for more than one marker, then the presumption of inequity would be stronger. Data does not always exist, in a comparative form, for all markers, or for all countries, or for strictly comparable groups. The comparisons that are critical are those between groups within a particular country, rather than between countries: for example, in Table 1 above, where the significance is not that Belgian first-generation migrants scored 415, Germans 440, and the UK 555, but that, comparing the gap between first generation scores and native scores in each country, the second generation score narrows the gap by just 15% in Belgium, the gap *increases* by 20% in Germany (German-born and educated children of migrants perform less well reading German than their migrant parents), and the gap is narrowed by 80% in the UK. What policies and practices work so well in the UK and much less well in Belgium? What causes second generation migrants in Germany to regress from the levels achieved by their parents? Markers that assess outcomes – during educational process, at the end of formal education, and at appropriate stages after this, allow policy makers, practitioners and communities to identify inequities, to target appropriate resources and activities, and to measure subsequent changes in outcomes. We set out our proposed markers below.

Literacy

The level of functional literacy achieved, at whatever age for which data was available, can be used as a proxy for attainment. Although some countries may not be producing comparative data between different groups for other curricular areas, or for combinations of standards reached in groups of subjects, this seemed to be the most ubiquitous measure. Figure 1 (above) shows some of the kinds of comparison that can be made, both within countries and, to a more limited extent, between countries.

Post compulsory education participation in education or training

The European Union's emphasis on achieving a highly educated workforce predicates a significant proportion of the population staying in education beyond compulsory schooling, either for further education or for training (as shown in Figure 2, above). This is sometimes associated with a category called NEET – the proportion of the young adults '*n*ot in *e*mployment, *e*ducation or *t*raining'. In terms of policies of social inclusion, any evidence that particular minorities were significantly less involved in education and training after the end of compulsory schooling would indicate significant disadvantage.

Higher Education

As part of the above, the continuing demand for a highly skilled and knowledgeable population (for 'the knowledge society') anticipates that a growing proportion of the population will enter higher education. Higher education can provide particularly significant access to professional occupations, to influence, power and social goods, and to better remunerated work. Yet in most European countries, admission to higher education is skewed in favour of particular socio-economic groups, and sometimes against ethnic and linguistic minorities and those with disabilities. There are also considerable gender disparities between different subjects. We therefore examine access to higher education as a marker of potential inequality.

Employment

Although educational systems are not provided merely to enable access to employment, most people expect one of the outcomes of successful education to be regular and satisfying employment. While the measurement of employment rates and occupational patterns of different groups will be indicative of potential larger societal discrimination, it will also indicate the level of educational success reached by members of a particular group.

School exclusion, social exclusion and bullying

Although schooling may be compulsory for particular periods, schools often have the ability to exclude pupils, on a temporary or even permanent basis. There is evidence that schools may sometimes exercise this on the basis of the willingness or not of the pupil to conform to particular behavioural expectations, and these sometimes involve bias or discrimination against what is seen as 'normal' or 'mainstream' behaviour or practice. Exclusion rates that are high for particular minority groups thus reveal both that some members of this group are not receiving a full education, and that there may be possible discrimination against cultural practices that are seen as 'not normal'

Such discrimination is not only sometimes instigated by schools when they exclude pupils, but is also carried out by other pupils against their peers, in the form of bullying and other forms of harassment. When this is targeted against particular minorities, it can damage the learning and study opportunities of those who are bullied. Where records are kept of incidents of bullying, evidence that members of particular minorities are proportionately more bullied than others again indicates that there is some educational disadvantage occurring.

Subject balance and other structural issues

Finally, in some instances educational systems apply, wittingly or unwittingly, structural barriers to access to educational provision that may give rise to inequalities to particular groups. Restricting access to certain types of schooling as 'academic', as opposed to 'vocational', for example, can in practice limit entry to higher status educational streams to members of particular socio-economic groups. In many cases, an early division of this kind can mean that a child who has started on the 'vocational' route will find it very difficult to switch to the 'academic' route, if at all. Such early setting into streams has important implications in potentially restricting later access to higher education (see above). There are also pressures of differential expectations of groups of pupils being used to affect subject choice – very commonly expressed examples of this function to restrict the entry of girls to scientific or technical subjects, but there are many others.

How do countries respond to evidence of educational disadvantages in their systems? In the next chapter, we look at two common responses: to deny that the problem really exists (evasion), or to acknowledge the existence of inequity, but to deny any responsibility for its cause, or its solution (evasions). In chapter five, we look at some of issues that arise when some countries attempt to tackle educational inequalities.

CHAPTER FOUR

EVASIONS AND EXCUSES

This book discusses the dilemmas in targeting educational inequalities, the use of poor measures of outcomes, and the use of evasions and excuses, which amount in some cases to doing very little or even total negligence. Laclau (1996) asserts that any country which claims to support a good society, for all its people, is one that exerts an ideology. The starting point for this chapter is that evasions and excuses are also the consequence of explicit or implicit ideologies. Excuses for continuing not to solve severe educational and social ills constitute a range of explanations. In some countries, government obligations to address inequity have increasingly been transferred to private providers, with the pronounced faith that solutions to any problem will, by definition, be better achieved through the private sector.

This has led in some cases to marketisation, with profit maximization as a goal, and social responsibility subordinated to economic interests. In one of the continuing examples used in this chapter, we will consider how the lack of adequate educational provision for groups of Roma children is excused as being their own fault. Explanations and evasions may refer to 'culture', or to earlier political decisions for which current politicians can disclaim responsibility. Yet other excuses involve the alleged lack of support given by parents to their children.

The 'school for all'

The research in our fourteen country study (EPASI, 2006-2008: see Box1 in chapter one) showed, through individual country reports, thematic analyses, case studies and project studies, that much has been done to make improvements for disadvantaged groups. However, evasions continue to be made about failures of policies that are directed towards disadvantaged individuals and groups, on all levels from local community and school level to regional or national levels.

The study clearly showed, as is discussed by Ross in the *Overall Report* (2009), that we are dealing with conflicts between systems of values. On the one hand most countries, albeit with varying ways of describing this in their respective policies, have similar overall idea and intentions about producing what might be called 'a school for all' – they may struggle to achieve this in different ways, but the goal is similar. Built into the meaning of 'a school for all' is the concept that schools can be envisioned as social meeting places. Children and young people from all kind of backgrounds meet and are educated in the same school and this, *per se*, is considered to be a key incentive for democratic education for all (Hartsmar 2008).

Most states within UNESCO signed the Salamanca declaration in 1994 (UNESCO 1994): this states that the signatories committed themselves to facilitate that students be taught together, regardless of various forms of difference, ability, gender or ethnic background. The 'school for all' concept rests on a strong belief in creating a democratic and equitable school, in which every student has the undisputed right to expect democracy and equity. Does this mean the same in every context? Does anyone have a greater right than another to interpret how democracy should be formed? It is more likely that an ideal that takes democratic values as its starting point will be constantly renegotiated by those involved, be they politicians, teachers or students. Biesta (2006) discusses the differences between what can be accomplished by 'Education *for* democracy' and 'Education *through* democracy' (112-114), and concludes that education through democracy is a specific way of educating for democracy, because it includes participation in democratic life.

In *Democracy and Education* (1966) Dewey observes that democracy has to be constantly discovered and rediscovered, shaped and reshaped and that democracy has a deeper meaning than government.

> A democracy is more than a form of government; it is primarily a mode of associated living, of conjoint communicated experience. The extension in space of the number of individuals who participate in an interest so that each has to refer his own action to that of others, and to consider the action of others to give point and direction to his own. (1966:199)

Laclau (2005) points out that the concept of a school for all cannot be filled with all its possible meanings, nor be open to challenge, until the time when different teachers - with all the resources each has available - try to translate ideology into practice..

Assarsson (2007) discusses the concept of a school for all in rhetorical terms, emphasising that equivalence is one of the signs that give meaning to the concept. She compares the school for all concept to:

a fluent significant that can encompass other signs, e.g. social, ethnical and gender discourses and discourses on special needs education. Within a discourse of equivalence these signs convey new meanings. Equivalence is dominated by a democratic discourse but in its materialisation teachers have to deal with a discursive antagonism of meanings in terms of accessibility for all children, individualization and efficient goal fulfilment. In this struggle between values, all equal in strength, the teachers handle dilemmas by reasoning on a pragmatic micro level. (252)

The market as an excuse for undermining welfare principles

At just the same time that we are developing the discourse of a school for all, founded on concepts of equity and justice and presented within a strong discourse of democracy, we are exposed to a neo-liberal market discourse, that emphasises freedom of choice, concerning for example parental choice over schools for their children, measurable targets, national and international testing and ranking systems, with a focus on core concepts like freedom of choice, competition and individualism (Cederberg, Hartsmar and Lingärde 2008; Leathwood *et al.* 2008; Nihad 2009; Olmeida Reinoso 2008; Ross 2009).

Beach (2008) problematises the emergence of more and more schools being driven by profit motives. He suggests that this might lead to some students being regarded negatively, of little value to the school, because they require more resources than for what is considered to be 'normal', but the meaning of 'normal' is seldom problematised.

Mitchell (2006) discusses some twenty years of the prevalent neo-liberal perspective on educational policies, and perceives what she terms a 'third way discourse'. She identifies links and interconnections to policies from a social democratic perspective. But this third way discourse is also framed by economic rationalities: 'the aims of social cohesion are firmly yoked to the ongoing neoliberal mantra of global competition' (48). Mitchell writes:

The third way rhetoric seems to promote a gentler, fairer government through partnerships and various methods of decentralized decision-making, but in effect these changes act to increase both individual and regional competition, devolve responsibility to specific 'agents' and to

further undermine welfarist principles of redistribution and responsibility.
(12-13)

In his book *När marknaden kom till förorten, valfrihet, konkurrens och symboliskt kapital i mångkulturella områdens skolor* [When the market came to the suburb: Choice, competition and symbolic capital in multicultural neighbourhoods' schools], Bunar (2008) gives an overview of international research and discussion on 'the freedom of choice' principle. He sets out various forms of levels of compliance, and various attitudes towards freedom of choice – from 'thoroughly good' to 'thoroughly bad', with hesitant and indeterminate positions between these – and concludes that the debate is characterised by ideological arguments rather than clear research. Bunar (107) quotes Bourdieu *et al* (1999): 'the truth is best expressed by those who have experienced it', interviewing chief education officers, headmasters and young people in metropolitan multicultural areas. His findings depict a range of multiple and diverse problems and negative attitudes towards what the interviewees consider to be the consequences of 'freedom of choice'. Bunar uses the concept of the 'logic of resignation', by which he means the explanatory model used by those working in schools characterised by diversity. The interviewees believe their own schools to be of good quality, at the same time expressing concern at the possibility that the Swedish-born students will, in a free market system, be lost to schools which show little or no diversity. There is a parallel political discussion to this, on whether politicians should interfere with this marketisation and the choices of parents and students. The political decision to let the market set the operational agenda for running schools has created a lack of symbolic capital in those schools that are characterised by diversity. This, says Bunar, underlines the weak competitiveness created, when compared to the more 'Swedish' schools.

In his book *Konkurrensens konsekvenser: Vad händer med svensk välfärd* [The consequences of competition. What is happening to Swedish welfare?] Vlachos (2011) describes the privatisation of health care and education that Sweden has undergone over the past two decades, describing it as unparalleled in scope and pace. He argues that these social changes were ideologically motivated. The differences between schools have increased: high-performing students from richer socio-economic backgrounds seek to attend what families describe as 'good' schools. These are often private schools, and Vlachos' conclusion is that, on average, outcomes have neither been improved nor worsened by the school reform. Fears that competition would lead to grade inflation and segregation can be seen in part. Vlachos claims that twenty years ago there was no research to suggest that schools in the private sector could have positive effects on quality and costs. But Hartman (2011) concludes that the state of knowledge on the consequences of privatisation for quality, costs and efficacy is remarkably limited. One might ask why there has been such little interest in looking for evidence for that these changes have had the desired effect?

Does 'all' mean 'all'?

Across Europe there is trend that students, regardless of their individual needs, are taught together in the same classrooms. While the number of resource centres supporting ordinary school work increases, the number of pupils in special schools diminishes. In *Key principles for Special Needs Education* (European Agency for Development in Special Needs Education 2003) comprehensive teaching is seen as an important basis for equal opportunities for persons *with special needs*, responsive to the individual students' diverse and often complex needs in all aspects of their lives.

However, it can also be seen that rather than offering the solutions required, politicians and education authorities sometimes choose to place students in educational groups where they do not belong. Vrabcova *et al* (2008:17) discuss the complexity of solving the long-term set of problems related to the profound poverty of the Roma community, given that the process of Czech democratization only started after the political changes of 1989. They show the inconsistencies in implementing politically decided measures about Roma children's schooling and their inclusion into majority society is impaired: between 60 and 80 percent of Roma children are placed in Special schools, originally intended to meet the needs of mentally handicapped children.

The same problem of grossly inappropriate school placements has been repeatedly reported in the Swedish media (for example, *Dagens Nyheter,* 2011). A study by the Skolinspektionen (2011a, The Swedish Schools Inspectorate) of some 1400 primary, secondary and upper-secondary schools in 2010 concluded that there were:

- deficiencies in the adaptation of teaching, leading to a deterioration of learning conditions;
- low trust and expectations of students' abilities;

- not enough support for students in special needs;
- insufficient monitoring of results;
- no continuous and systematic quality assurance; and
- little preparation for actions against abusive treatment.

Lack of support for students in special needs was studied in 30 municipalities in Sweden, with a focus on placements in compulsory and upper secondary schools for students with learning disabilities (Skolinspektionen 2011b). The Swedish Education Act requires that children normally attend a mainstream primary school. Only children with developmental disabilities, mental retardation or brain damage (and thus with severe learning disabilities) are entitled to attend special schools. A special school is thus not intended to cater for *all* children who need support: the elementary school is expected to be responsible to give all children the support they need. Yet the proportion of pupils in special schools has increased over the past fifteen years, from about 1.0 percent per academic year 1995/96 to 1.4 percent in 2009/2010.

This failure to conduct an adequate diagnosis of the specific levels of learning need, and instead allocating a child who should not be there to a special school, has major implications for the child's possibility of further study in the future. After completing basic school or upper secondary special school, there will be fewer opportunities to progress to vocational or other types of training. The decision to assign a child to a special school or not, is in many ways critical to the child's future: the procedure must be correct, and the investigation complete and of good quality. The School Inspectorate identifies two crucial problems.

Firstly, investigations are characterised by missing lacking information, particularly about social and medical issues. In most cases it is impossible to determine, from the investigations made and their findings, whether the child should attend special school or not. The quality of management and supporting evidence for a decision is insufficient for an assessment. All 30 municipalities in the study were criticised, and were subsequently required to re-investigate the position of each child then attending special schools. There was a strong concern that there are children put in special schools for the wrong reasons.

Secondly, the report shows that the proportion of pupils with foreign backgrounds is higher in special schools than in elementary school. Schools Inspectorate Report did not conclude what caused this difference.

There were concerns that the municipalities' lack of diagnostic techniques led to misinterpretions of the problems these pupils encounter, which resulted in them being sent to special schools. They concluded this to be an extremely serious issue requiring further study: students who have been sent inappropriately to special schools should have the opportunity and support to acquire further education.

A question of credibility

Examining the position of Roma students in special schools in the Czech Republic, Vrabcova *et al.* (2008:9) observed that 'the local urban authorities often have neither financial resources nor motivation to improve the situation of these Roma groups.' They reported, for example, that while schools and teachers are supposed to teach health and hygiene issues, a quarter of the Roma children were living below the poverty line without running water in their home environment. There is a conflict of legitimacy and a credibility gap. Evasions about not targeting the basic living circumstances of a severely disadvantaged group, coupled with excuses for not finding appropriate school placements, will, we argue, lead to establishing disadvantage and exclusion, and thus continued educational disadvantage in the country. The European policy review on education, *EU Research in Social Sciences and Humanities,* argues that education policies initiatives can only have limited effects on issues such as integration, so long as they are not linked to wider social policies and economic reforms. In other words, inaction on one front can allow action on another front to appear to have an effect, but that this is just a superficial cosmetic.

The OECD report *Starting Strong II, Early Childhood Education and Care* (2006:206) underlines this:

> The reduction of child and family poverty is a precondition for successful early childhood care and education systems. Early childhood services do much to alleviate the negative effects of disadvantage by educating young children and facilitating the access of families to basic services and social participation. However, a continuing high level of child and family poverty in a country undermines these efforts and greatly impedes the task of raising educational levels. Governments need to employ upstream fiscal, social and labour policies to reduce family poverty and give young children a fair start in life.

Ziegler *et al.* (1996) and Dearing *et al.* (2006) conclude that it is not sufficient to provide care and education to children from any 'at-risk' group: a good outcome is only attainable if structural poverty and institutional discrimination are also addressed.

Similarly, a Position Paper on social inclusion by Eurocities Network (2000: 3) argues

> Eurocities strongly advocates to politically defining social exclusion as a dynamic process, in which not only the affected groups and their living circumstances are targeted, but the causes, the agents and mechanisms of exclusion as well. Inclusion policies to promote the full participation in society are only successful if the obstacles that block their access are done away with, if the causes of exclusion are removed, the agents change their attitudes and practices and the mechanisms of exclusion disappear.

The obvious - and more challenging and long term - measures are around the concern about why authorities 'lack motivation' (as Vrabcova *et al.* (2008) put it) to target the lack of basic facilities. As Hargreaves (2003) points out, teachers have to navigate in the collision between the steering documents directive and a complex reality.

In countries such as France 'some minorities, like gypsies or disabled people, do have rights but educational policies have not met their needs so far' (Étienne *et al* 2008, p. 14; also Liégeois 2007). In Greece, Spinthourakis *et al.* (2008) report the same problems of 'paper reforms failing to have bearing on reality'. Dooly and Vallejo (2008) point out how the Spanish Roma community is categorised as a minority ethnic group, similar to recent immigrants, despite their having had Spain as a homeland for centuries. This evasion of recognising an indigenous minority clearly goes against the European *Framework Convention for the Protection of National Minorities* (Council of Europe, 2009).

This dilemma of 'paper reforms' is reflected in a recurring global educational discourse of ambivalence, between valuing education on the one hand as a social and democratic movement and on the other hand as an economic investment that does not provide adequate returns (see chapter two). Trondman (2009:242) summarises the situation:

> In other words, it seems that more and more poor children from increasingly segregated neighbourhoods go to increasingly unequal schools showing deteriorating school performance and impaired health. Political reform and techniques for control seems to me not only reinforce these trends, but also make children more responsible for managing their own vulnerability.

In an historical and social perspective, schools can be seen as institutions devoted to legitimise and perpetuate societal power relations, principally by sorting students into aptitudes for different future working positions. This legitimising function holds a position above the pedagogical one. From the examples given above, and from a power perspective (Foucault, 1986), the way in which the majority group's cultural heritage is conveyed to all students as the acceptable 'normal way of how we do things' can be seen as both a form of implicit control and the establishment of what is acceptable or not. Although the curricula in many countries may formally stress the importance of making several perspectives available in teaching controversial issues, this appears to have little bearing on reality. Finding excuses for not taking action against social structural problems inhibits addressing the underlying causes, as well as preventing the achievement of possible solutions for the exposed groups.

The era of the problem children

Nirje (1970; 1980; 1999) put forward a widely recognised normalisation principle, which had as its starting point the ideal of equality, aiming to achieve decent and tolerable living conditions for all citizens. As an example of this, the Swedish Social Services Act (LSS Socialstyrelsen. Lag om stöd och service till vissa funktionshindrade) provides personal support services to people in need, based on the principle of the right to a dignified life – for example, to be able to get out of bed, to feed oneself, to travel and to maintain contact with others, regardless of age, residence or individual economic circumstances. Despite the intentions of Social Services Act, cases have been reported of local municipalities interpreting the Act by arguing that the individual is primarily responsible for paying this, rather than the municipality. This allows the municipality to avoid financial responsibility, and means that poorer clients are unable to utilise the personal support services to which they are entitled.

This normalisation discussion has been extended to include special education, creating a conceptual distinction between categorical and relational perspectives when talking about individuals in special needs (Skidmore (1996), Clark, Dyson and Millward (1998) and (Emanuelsson, Persson and Rosenqvist (2001)). A categorical perspective approach makes the classification of students in special needs based on contrasting them with the normal. The alternative relational perspective requires any discussion about students in difficulty to focus on the interplay between the individual and the surrounding society.

Emanuelsson, Persson and Rosenqvist (2001) suggest that even if the influence of a wider relational perspective can be seen, previous research overviews have predominantly worked within a categorical approach perspective, and that this is part of a general international pattern. The outcomes of studies located within such a paradigm are that findings are medically based and psychological, and offer very little support in using such knowledge directly in teaching contexts. The authors underline the importance of using special needs skills in research that aims to understand the wider educational context. The proportion of those who are considered deviant (or 'non-normal') in any given community is determined by the social construction of normality, and the conception of the societally normal stigmatises those considered deviant. The assumption that 'we' are normal creates varieties of discrimination, through which 'we' effectively, if often unthinkingly, reduce the life chances of individuals in this stigmatised category (Goffman 1963:14).

Emanuelsson *et al* conclude that the appearance of direct market-related values and conditions in special needs education is correlated with the processes of the administrative decentralisation of provision, and the increased opportunities for 'free' choices that are characteristic of contemporary education policy (2001:145). They argue that if measures are not taken an important consequence will be significant and increasing differences between various schools. These differences are usually decisive in determining the 'market value' of specialist teacher training and its use. When the categorical and individual focussed perspective is dominant, these conditions become hidden or suppressed, while they may appear more evident within a relational perspective.

Börjesson and Palmblad (2003) describe four categories in distinguishing actions taken to differentiate and exclude school children from mainstream 'normal' education. In the first group are the physically ill and disabled, who are often placed in schools outside the regular school system. Children described as disruptive, unruly and disobedient and with disturbed concentration represent a second group. These children may often be diagnosed as 'having' ADHD, etc. (see also Hartsmar 2008). Thirdly are children who do not make 'normal' progress in their learning, who are consequently placed in special education groups or in special schools for children with learning disabilities. The fourth group consists of children who have been bullied or victimised, who are often removed from their school to other parts of the school, or even to a different school, because the school uses the excuse that they have exhausted all other possibilities. Although this is intended to protect the child, it may result in the bullied student having to eat lunch away from the rest of the class, spending the break in the staff room, and having an assistant on guard against further violations. Such a response and support may create temporary calm, but it can also contribute to increased exclusion: consequently the bullied students may feel even more singled out and exposed. Sometimes the school tries to solve the situation with setting work that can be carried out at home, or homeschooling. This leads to much less contact with teachers and peers. One might cynically note the school in this hides the problem rather than solves it: what you cannot see does not exist.

Begler points out that some schools' lame excuses of having exhausted all options ends with the student effectively expelled, missing schooling through these changes and interruptions: the bullies have triumphed again (*Aftonbladet,* 2011, 'Mobbade elever blir dubbelt kränkta' [Bullied students end up doubly offended]), Though the school may feel that the immediate problem is solved, the underlying causes, both the bully and the bullied, are in many cases neglected and evaded. Cederberg (2011) points to the conclusion in a Government report (SOU 2010: 64) 'The negative experience in school is therefore an intermediary, a link that has a very special significance for the future outcome. What happens at school can thus be problematic, but is also something that can be changed by means of educational and social activities.' School itself may constitute a strong risk factor for vulnerable children.

Power structures and the sorting of children

This sorting of children into categories of normal and abnormal can, in historical and social perspective, be seen as part of the process by which institutions legitimate and perpetuate societal power relations by sorting students into different future working positions. This legitimising function holds a position superior to the pedagogical role. From a power perspective (Foucault 1986), conveying the majority group's cultural heritage and expectations to students - that it should be accepted as the 'normal' way of how 'we' do things - can be seen as both implicit control and the establishment of what is beyond the acceptable. Since normality can be considered to be a social construction, the definition of deviation has varied over time. Foucault analyses the relationship between deviation and normality and argues that what characterises rationality and irrationality is bound to specific historical and social formations. Reason is, according to Foucault, a power factor exercised by the rational and used to oppress and isolate the irrational. The boundary between children in special needs and those who are not can therefore mainly be understood as a social construction. It is not only a question of who exercises power, how they do this, what is not done and what the consequences are for the individuals involved. Foucault is discussing how identities are formed, which identities are allowed to come into the foreground and which are made impossible and expelled into the periphery.

Over the last decade there has been a tendency to clarify and stress the significance of teachers' pedagogical work, from early childhood onwards. McLeod and Fettes (2007) showed that school failure among students with mental health problems was linked to school failure to offer support activities that worked for the group. There were conflicts between teachers and children and children and their peers and low expectations of what students described as having special needs might be capable or achieve. Hamre and Pianta (2005) showed that at-risk children increased their school performance and changed their earlier unfavourable behaviour when efforts were made to create a strong, emotionally supportive learning environment with improved personal relationships between teacher and child. Stipek and Miles (2008) found that teachers could develop good relationships with students by continuing to communicate high expectations, by giving attention to positive behaviour and through continued dialogue. They suggest that there is a correlation between students' conflicts with teachers, aggressive behaviour and pupils' poorer performance in school. Having no or very low expectations, instead of meeting the student with trust in an emotionally strong environment has been shown to be of crucial importance. The logical consequence of not having any expectations of some students is that schools do not then need to provide necessary support functions, because they are not considered worthwhile.

There may well be no single or 'best' way to categorise or work with individuals or groups, but we argue there are possibilities for effecting change. The imperative is to be intentionally open to alternative and diverse explanations, possibilities and other eventualities. A plurality of explanations and understandings are necessary, together with a critical scrutiny of existing taken-for-granted discourses.

Emanuelsson; Persson and Rosenqvist (2001) comment that traditional special education often commences after the distinction and categorisation of 'special children' has already been made, usually after teaching within mainstream 'normal' conditions. In other words, the education that is given to those in such a category is structured around the notion of the 'special', with an often unconsciously formulated intention to make them 'more normal' and thus able to return to mainstream education. However well-intentioned such an approach to the 'special', one result clearly is that there is no need to adjust or change the regular curriculum or regular classroom practice, since this is considered to be the 'normal' state to which the special should aspire to rejoin.

Some researchers and commentators have pointed to what might be called a battle of ideologies. Holmberg, in *Skola och Samhälle SOS* [School and Society, 2011], comments on what he calls a debate disguised as a book about the history of schooling. He analyses *Mot bättre vetande – en svensk skolhistoria* (Larsson 2011; [Against better Judgement – a Swedish school history]) as a neo-liberal perspective on educational development that goes hand-in-hand with political conservatism. Larsson criticises what he describes as teachers becoming the 'creators of social harmony' instead of following what he takes to be their proper role, of 'communicating knowledge'. Holmberg claims that Larsson focuses criticism of mainstream schooling when he claims that the Social Democrats have what he terms a misguided concern for 'weakly motivated kids' and 'the school-weary', and that this has led to the undifferentiated, unified school. 'Burnout' and 'weakly motivated' children are now taught in the same classes as their 'more gifted' peers.

Holmberg compares Larsson's work to the contributions to the educational debate of Enkvist, In *Feltänkt - en kritisk granskning av idébakgrunden till svensk utbildningspolitik* (2000) [Thinking errors – a critical review of the idea background to Swedish education policy] Enkvist asserts that a particular ideology has destroyed the Swedish school and teacher education: She claims that schooling is in decay because there is a lack of discipline amongst students who don't want to learn, a misinterpretation of the meaning of democracy in schools and teachers who (she alleges) have abdicated from their role of being educators. The book is, Holmberg says,

> a stupendously conservative 'settling up' with the educational policy, the educational system, school and teacher education. It is stupendous because it has no social analysis. No changes in school are related to changes in society. The author finds it incomprehensible that the school looks different today than it did in the 1950s, when she asserts that it was at its best. Developments since then should have been halted. The implicit idea

basic to the book is this: the more people who acquire education/training, the lower the quality becomes and the more devalued is the value of education. It is a classical idea in a conservative world. (translated by present authors)

How have texts like this by Enkvist and others had any effect on school policies? One trend is that - instead of discussing better ways of supporting children and young people from disadvantaged backgrounds - more media commentators claiming that not all young people want a theory-based education. They should not be required to stay in school if they are not sufficiently able or motivated, and should instead be directed towards vocational training. But doing so at too early a stage may in its turn lead to fewer possibilities for change later in life. This could be seen as a barely concealed ideology of 'shoemaker, stick to your last'. The hierarchical dichotomy between 'theoretical' and 'practical' education makes it possible to maintain existing social stratification instead of using schooling as a key mechanism enabling democratic education for all. The ideological rational explains that those who fail in school do so because of personal and social inferiority: they have no aptitude for learning (Rose 1994).

Avoiding making necessary social analyses, and evading the use of intersectionality to scrutinise social issues in schooling, makes it easier to criticize schools, teachers and students. Lykke (2005:8) points out that society largely consists of interacting socio-cultural hierarchies and various power structures, and that if it is not taken into account that schools have very similar structures it becomes easier to excuse the re-creation of a highly segregated school. Indiscriminately talking about groups instead of individuals (such as immigrants, Roma, Muslims, handicapped, boys, students *with* special needs, and so on) can become a way of evading acknowledging the potential of each individual. Identity categories, such as Roma or immigrants, interact with hierarchies of class and ethnicity. But that which can be seen as subordination in one context can be seen as superiority in another, or both can exist and interact simultaneously. When a student is diagnosed as a person *with* special needs this indicates that the issue is a personal one. But an alternative approach would be to refer to students *in* difficulties. This reflects an acknowledgment of structural societal problems. Just as not making services such as public transport, restaurants and shops available to all, so restricting access to school and university by not taking everyone's educational needs into account exposes the individual to special problems and creates their special needs.

The shibboleth as separator between 'us' and 'them'

The original shibboleth referred to a linguistic feature that was used by the Gileadites to identify the Ephraimite enemies. The Ephramites could not pronounce the initial 'sh' in Shibboleth (Judges 12). Shibboleths are now often used to separate the customs and traditions of one group from those of another one. An in-joke is typically a way of telling others that this can only be understood by 'us'. Strong beliefs in the superiority of traditions and customs of one group compared to another, such as living in a house compared to a mobile home, also function to affirm an individual as a member of a community and serves as a distinguishing shibboleth and an identification of, for example, one's social status or regional origin.

Do we want all groups to be included on equal terms? On the one hand, educating citizens enables those in power to spread their dominant culture with their beliefs, traditions, knowledge and ethics. On the other hand, education can give new insights and an opportunity to question the prevailing normativity. Those who do not have the same beliefs, or eat the same foods, or use different clothes, or do not want to work as many hours as 'we' do become the unassimilated, the unintegrated: 'the other'. Considering such cultural norms as being a particular group's fault can become a political excuse for not doing more for them – for example, the Roma population. 'They don't want to change and become like the rest of us'. Identifying with a belief that would be difficult for anyone outside a given group's view or ideology to accept becomes a good example of a political shibboleth. Kamali (2006) shows how a persistent housing segregation also creates a kind of mental separation, which supports concepts of 'the other' as marginalised and, in the absence of status, the inferior.

Let's pretend that everyone gets the password to the 'school for all' door – what then?

In previous sections we have discussed the hindrances and excuses used do deny everyone access to a school for all. In this final section we will discuss the didactic implications behind excusing the planning for a school for all. In one sense, one *can* say that a school for all really does exists, and this is connected with how much education is carried out. In a research review, Hartsmar and Jönsson (2010) show that evading identifying the student as an individual within a group has implications on two levels.

Firstly, their review raises four didactic questions: *Who* are the children? *What* are they to study? *Why* are they to study this specific content and *how* can it be carried out? The questions who, what and why are only dealt with in a marginal way: goals are not discussed in relation to the importance of particular content for particular children. So, first and foremost, students' experiences, backgrounds, interests and needs are neglected.

In a study that involved interviewing teachers about history teaching (Hartsmar 2001), the teachers often used lack of time as an excuse for not acknowledging the diversity in the classroom, or for not reflecting upon why they only plan the familiar and secure.

> I hardly dare to give the answer, because I think it's typical for many teachers. One is steered by the teaching material. I'm relying a lot on the book, actually. /.../ It is totally a question of ambition. Maybe my notions are preconceived but I think that if you want to go deeply into history teaching you should spend a considerable amount of time. (Male teacher, year 5) (Hartsmar 2001: 224: translated by the present authors)

This response (and other similar responses) should be considered in relation to what is of great importance in developing historical consciousness: taking a starting point in the students' various experiences and expectations, letting them voice a diversity of perspectives and relating their perspectives to the past, the present and the future.

The second implication of Hartsmar and Jönsson's review (2010) is that most of the instruction in most school subjects is characterised by a canonical, uncontested textbook-bound content, that does not link to the students who will follow this. The few times that – from a pedagogical perspective - the issue of *who* was foregrounded in the interviews, it concerned students who were said to have problems with 'normal' schoolwork. The main focus is on educational methods, and a discourse of promoting homogeneity and normalisation emerges.

When the *how* question dominates, this is usually with the aim of making the traditional subject more attractive through developing teaching methods that encourage student engagement. They are often allowed to choose between a whole battery of methods, and may also select the order in which they do things.

Why does the *who* question have the weakest place in didactical considerations? As stated above, many international policy documents explicitly assert that individuals and groups of children bring a variety of experiences and needs, and that these need to become the focus for the group. Such documents place the child clearly in the foreground. But why do so few educationalists and researchers consider and clarify the question about *who*? Why isn't, the construction of identity taken more into account in a multi-contextual period of childhood and youth, and why are children and young people not encouraged to assume the role of active participants in an increasingly complex society?

Using the experiences of children and young people as a starting point mean that the teacher (broadly, using a variety of sources) must be familiar with the social environment of the children in the group, and the various experiences and needs they can be assumed to have. For example, Comber (2001) demonstrates the importance of the teacher being informed with up-to-date knowledge about the society and area they are active in. Teachers, Comber maintains, need broad, multi-faceted knowledge from different sources. With this as a foundation, one can better understand the individual child's experiences and needs.

Instead of talking about 'the experiences of children', the concepts of the *child perspective* and the *child's perspective* are used by Halldén (2003:21). She discusses and problematises the ambiguities in the concept of a child perspective, which she says has ideologically been afforded a large 'rhetorical capacity'. To assume a child perspective can, in our interpretation, be put on the same level as curriculum directives and equated to the wider knowledge of society and conditions that Comber (2001) describes. Broadly speaking, these have their basis not only in the various life conditions, experiences and needs of children, but also in listening to individual children and interpreting what they express in a discursive context. To allow the child's perspective to be expressed is to allow the individual child to express his experiences, intentions, interests, needs and opinions. This should not be interpreted as a promotion of egocentrism, where children are only interested in what they themselves have to say: rather it is a way of promoting democratic education in cooperation with others.

Hannah Arendt (2004:228) asserts that in order to act, we need others responding to the initiatives we take: acting is not possible without plurality. As soon as we deny plurality we distance ourselves from the others' particularity. Instead of seeing human subjectivity as an attribute, Arendt defines it as a characteristic in human interaction. Humans cannot be subjects in isolation. We become subjects when our initiatives are not hindered by others.

Biesta (2006) draws on Arendt's social and political conception of the democratic person and puts the following questions to educators: What kind of schools do we need in order for students to be able to act? To what extent, is acting possible in schools? On the one hand, Biesta (124-126) says it requires an educational environment in which students are allowed to take initiatives. It also requires an educational environment that does not just focus on the reproduction of curricula content, transmitted from teachers to students: it requires a view of language as something necessary for human interaction. With reference to Arendt, (2004:209), Biesta (2006:129) concludes:

> Since subjectivity not only occurs or is created in school it moves the responsibility for democratic education back to where it belongs, to society as a whole. It is an illusion to believe that schools themselves on their own can produce democratic citizens.

Teachers and schools need, we argue, politicians and educational authorities to allow them real possibilities for democratic education and to trust them to manoeuvre between the specific experiences, backgrounds, interest and needs of their students.

CHAPTER FIVE

THE DILEMMAS OF TARGETING INEQUALITY

In his biting criticism of 'imperialistic' democracy and free trade, McLaren (2010) describes how a new notion of social justice allows for rampant inequality as long as it confines itself to capitalist social relations. According to the author, through the escalation of capitalism's two original axes – deregulation and privatization – inequity has been allowed to expand throughout far-reaching social domains, including education and knowledge production.

> Sadly, in the academy, and especially in institutions of graduate education, the challenge to capitalism has not taken place in the realm of material life, but rather in the arena of discourse and the politics of representation. (McLaren, 2010: 196)

As we have discussed in chapter two, economic theories are key elements in the development of educational policies and subsequent practices. It has even been argued that low socio-economic status may be an underlying factor for the majority of disadvantaged groups (chapter three). In a similar vein to McLaren, Macrine, Hill and Kelsh (2010) argue that class has been occluded in mainstream educational theory in order to legitimate the property relations constituting capitalism and that this is a root cause of exploitation, domination, and oppression (p. 2). Along the lines of other theorists looking at the ways in which economic status intersects with other factors, they maintain that capitalism need not be understood only as an economic concept – cultural capital (or *habitus,* Bourdieu, 1971, 1974; Bourdieu and Passeron, 1990) has a pervasive role in determining educational curricula, policy and practice as well as access to this particular form of capital, as we analysed in our first chapter.

This is not to say that equal access to educational opportunities is deliberately and patently blocked for some and open for others. However, as long as 'knowledge production' and its representation is controlled by one particular group (McLaren, 2010), access to that knowledge is limited for anyone excluded from the 'knowledge-holders'. As it is has been underscored throughout this book, freedom of choice and 'equal opportunities', at closer glance, may not be as equitable as is often assumed. As Macrine, Hill and Kelsh contend:

> the choices members of either class make in the course of their daily lives –what they eat, where they live, whether and where they seek an education– are shaped by these bas(e)ic and inequitable production (property) relations. Class, in other words, determines social, political, and intellectual inequity. (2010: 2)

This blurring of lines between social justice and injustice – injustice becoming justifiable within specific capitalistic domains – implies inherent difficulties when it comes to finding solutions to situations of inequity in education. The exact meaning of words like 'choice' begins to be elusive. Even the identification of groups at risk – a necessary and meritorious step in order to quantify the inequity, to target resources and programmes, and to assess the effectiveness (if any) of the impact of such targeting – may become problematic. This notion of group selection has been introduced in chapter three and will be discussed in more detail in the chapter.

At the same time, when discussing inequity in education, it is important to maintain a perspective that does not focus on specific educational agents (students, teachers, parents, administrators, policy-makers, voters) as a sole cause for low achievement, low self-esteem, low motivation, and other consequences of a highly complex, interrelated, inequitable system, as is an educational organization. It is tempting to call into play the 'Complexity Theory' whose proponents state that systems are best regarded as wholes; the traditional emphasis on simplification and reduction is deemed as inadequate for understanding inherently nonlinear interconnected systems. The agency of actors in social systems cannot be ignored – individuals not only have room for self-determination, their activities can affect the larger society (system) – bringing us back to the point that power and knowledge are two aspects of the same process. The fact that social systems carry information about themselves and their environments implies that individuals are able to act on such information (Marion, 1999), and even possibly change the social systems that are acting on: this is what differentiates social systems from natural science systems.

Hardman (2010) argues that the applicability of theory of complexity to social systems is most useful if considered not from the point of view of complexity of the system but rather from the limitations of understanding or predicting the outcomes of human and (system) environment interaction. By placing focus on 'emergence', the complicit nature of agents (in this case, educational stakeholders) and their possibility of dynamically affecting the system (Davis and Sumara, 2006) is underlined; indeed Hardman (2010) goes one step further and poses that the individual can affect *meaning* within dynamic systems, as in the case of 'equal access to opportunities'.

The way in which 'obvious' (naturalised) discourse becomes embedded within the dynamic systems is almost impossible to trace, however, these 'collective understandings' are not top-down impositions, they emerge through the intersectionality of multiple sets of social relations within the dynamic systems. Walby (2007) calls for a theorization of the intersectionality of multiple, complex social inequalities. This allows for a more complete theorization of:

> the ontological depth of each set of social relations. Rather than there being merely a single base to each of these sets of social relations, there is a much deeper ontology, including the full range of domains: economy, polity, violence nexus, and civil society. Within each domain (economy, polity, violence, civil society), there are multiple sets of social relations (e.g. gender, class, ethnicity) (Walby, 2007: 454).

Similarly, Manuel-Navarette (2003) argues that social systems are actually nested hierarchies that are made up of many different structures such as

> structures of communication, systems of meaning, or discourse, ideologies, roles of individuals ..., power relations, values, individual perceptions, technology, knowledge, configurations of energy, matter, money, information fluxes, human time allocation structures, rituals, and others (2003: 12).

Arguably, then, the construction of power relations, individual and collective ideologies and values, representations of knowledge is directly tied to the 'systems of meaning' – displayed in the everyday social discourse.

Thus, this chapter aims to describe objects of knowledge (i.e. educational social systems) which have both discursive and non-discursive conditions of existence. By considering the intersectionality of multiple social inequalities as they naturally emerge – yet unpredictably through non-linear interactions – we may be able to better comprehend potential problems inherent to policies that identify and isolate underachieving groups. This chapter will first consider the discursive constructs of diversity and how its meaning may affect and be affected by the dynamics of the complex education system. Next, we describe how individual agency can influence the system's dynamics, in particular looking at decisions and actions that may lead to a cycle of segregation and downgrading of educational opportunities for specific groups of students. Finally, we consider how intersubjectivity, lending itself to the social construction of shared meanings, may create circumstances of inequality within the educational system.

Discursive links between diversity and inequity

In order to approach the questions of why and how educational systems fail to address equalities of outcome it is imperative to first consider how diversity is understood within different social discourses, thus highlighting the intersectionality of discourse in different sets of social relations. Trying to identify the existence of minority groups is itself fraught with inherent difficulties (see chapter three and four). In most educational domains (perhaps especially in policies), diversity is frequently coupled with the notion of minority groups (immigrants, heritage language students, minority ethnic or religious groups, etc.), leaving out members of majority groups. This implies that the majority group is not diverse and that diversity is constituted only of 'others' in addition to the majority.

In a report for OECD report, Burns and Shadoian-Gersing (2010: 21) provide a working definition of diversity as 'characteristics that can affect the specific ways in which developmental potential and learning are realised, including cultural, linguistic, ethnic, religious and socio-economic differences' (21). The OECD report upholds that there is an implicit distinction between diversity and disparity. Diversity is defined as a neutral concept that entails the richness of human experience (i.e. one can be thin, tall, near-sighted, etc.). Disparity, on the other hand, refers to sundry characteristics associated with different outcomes or differential treatment.

Still, the OECD report highlights the fact that the way in which diversity is understood and approached must be understood within contextually-bound parameters. For instance, countries which, historically, have been host to varying volumes and periods of immigration may tend to construct views of diversity as a strong background to a unified single identity (e.g. the motto of the United States of America: *e pluribus unum* ('of many, one')) or, as in the case of Canada, promote a multicultural, multilingual collective identity (a 'cultural mosaic', Burns and Shadoian-Gersing, 2010: 22).

In countries where immigration (on a relatively large scale) is seen as a rather new phenomenon, the idea of diversity may be constructed in a different manner from the ones described in the previous paragraph. Newly arrived cultures are expected to integrate and eventually assimilate into an assumedly unchanged single national identity (an identity that does not include possibilities of other cultural traits apart from those traditionally associated with the nation).

> Immigrants to these countries may be seen as presenting a challenge, to both the educational infrastructure and the national identity, and also can raise questions about who can 'be' a citizen. (...) Some of the countries that acceded to the Union in 2004, while not having, as yet, issues of immigration, also are sometimes reluctant to admit to difference and differentiation within their population. These policies make it hard to identify accurately where inequalities occur in education, or their extent. (Ross, 2009: 35)

It is understandable that newly-arrived students or first-generation students often face difficulties in their schooling due to obvious challenges such as learning a new language (or languages), adjusting to as new culture and social structure of the host country, and adjusting to an unfamiliar school system (Stanat and Christensen, 2006) and community, apart from the emotional toil of leaving their homeland. It stands to reason, however, that second-generation students should fare better than the first generation. These students were born in the host country, grew up speaking the native language and did not need to become accustomed to a new culture and social structure. However data from PISA 2003 and 2006 contradicts this (see also chapter three).

> This overall pattern is particularly troubling as it appears that in a number of countries second-generation students do not perform as well as their 'native' peers even though these students were also born and raised in the country. It is also remarkable because, while this is the average across all participating countries, in a number of countries immigrant students perform as well as their native born peers (e.g. Australia, Canada and New Zealand) (Burns and Shadoian-Gersing, 2010: 24).

So why are some disadvantaged groups, all with similar characteristics, doing better than others? This incongruence may be explained by the dialogic interaction taking place around the policies and practices aimed at 'diversity'. Diversity is often depicted as something to promote (see, for instance, the Common European Framework of Reference for Languages, 2001) while at the same time, it is often described as the root of educational and social inequality.

Moreover, political and social policies may broadly represent educational situations that are of current interest and which are being promoted by the state. When 'diversity' is a 'buzzword' policies aimed at ensuring equality with diverse groups may mushroom. This allows the government to be represented as an agency of change, working in the interests of all people wherein 'the people' are understood in terms of (multiple) cultural and social identity/ies, even when the representation is being manoeuvred from within the dominant ideological framework (Kumar, 2010).

Teachers, students, and policy-makers alike should be made aware of the ways in which multiple identities and diversity may be interwoven into an educational agenda aimed at the reproduction of cultural and social capital in a neo-liberal competitive model. Moreover, educational stakeholders must be able to recognise the way in which diversity may result in injustice (even racism) within the education system (Cole and Maisuria, 2010). Assuming that all public discourses are products of the society in which they are formulated there is an inherent risk that dominant discourses (e.g. those of the government, of big business, of large sections of the media, of the hierarchy of some trade unions) will directly reflect the interests of the ruling class rather than 'the general public' (Jenks, 2005); interests of minority groups are less likely to be represented in dominant discourse. For instance, aligning all disadvantaged groups under the label of diversity may mask the way in which categories intersect with each other.

> Sometimes, for example, ethnic minority categorisation conceals socio-economic disadvantage. (...) It may be simpler for governments to attribute inequalities to poverty than to acknowledge more complex patterns of discriminatory behaviour towards disadvantaged groups. (Ross, 2009: 37)

Inevitably, however, the identification of groups at risk is a necessary step in order to quantify inequity, to target resources and programmes, and to assess the effectiveness of the impact of such targeting, but the categorising of such groups can lead to further discrimination. Being aware that there is diversity within diversity may be an important first step. In a recent study of ESL (English as a Second Language) students in

Canada, the variegated backgrounds of the homogeneous ESL grouping were highlighted due to their significance to the data results:

> [D]ecision-makers must be careful to disaggregate data and use them critically when making judgments. Specifically, 'immigrant' or 'ESL' labels mask tremendous variation among the groups they subsume. In this study, Chinese speaking students performed extraordinarily well, and generally inflated the apparent achievement of other ESL ethno-cultural groups. Indeed, three of these ethno-cultural groups attained significantly lower outcomes than native English speakers. Teacher-educators are encouraged to make their teacher candidates aware of such variation, and that the challenges and advantages of one immigrant group may be far different than those experienced by another. (Garnett, 2010: 107)

Variegation is also an important issue when it comes to testing. Standardised tests, which are context-less with respect to the diversity of national educational cultures and curricula (Cederberg, Hartmann, and Lingärde, 2009), may produce negative washback on teachers, students and schools. For instance low achievement in testing may result in 'punishment' of schools and students (using achievement rates as a threat to reduce resources and spending rather than implementing measures for improvement). Discursively, making the schools and teachers responsible for the testing results provides a means for administrators and policy-makers to demonstrate that they are taking action (acting as agents of change). However, poorly resourced educational opportunities will negatively affect students' performance on tests and the cycle continues, as these students become further removed from the educational process.

Too low results in standardised testing (in which the design of the test does not take into consideration the immediate context of type and means of learning that has taken place (Popham, 2002)) often causes devastating emotional effects on both students and teachers. Students who have done poorly on standardised tests are more likely to become disillusioned and less motivated –leading to a vicious cycle of negative emotions towards learning in general (Haladyna, 2002; Dooly, Vallejo and Unamuno, 2009). (The dialogic links between being labelled as low-achievers and self-fulfilling prophecy are examined more closely later on in this chapter; self-fulfilling prophecy and teacher expectations are also examined in chapter three.) This link is not limited to low-achieving students. Teachers may become discouraged by results, may feel pressured by administration and media and they may begin to blame, or at least feel that their students are incapable of improving their scores in standardised testing. Kohn (2005) has argued that when students fail to perform at standard levels, teachers typically provide a very conditional acceptance of them, as only the high scoring students are congratulated and respected (Kohn, 2005). In other words, the 'emergence' of new elements in the complex system (low achievement results, media pressure, low motivation) will contribute to the multiple complex social inequalities (Walby, 2007: 454).

Another way in which intellectual (or educational) inequity may be perpetuated is through 'the general discourse of meritocracy (…), the argument that all that is necessary is a system in which 'the best' can 'rise' to the top' (Ross, 2009:15; see also chapter three). 'It is a myth that it is possible for everyone to move up the ranks on the basis of hard work, fortitude, and perseverance. This justifies the social division of labour and class differentiation and mystifies the agonistic relation among the classes' (Kumar, 2010: 82).Groups that have access to the desired cultural capital will be at an advantage when it comes to 'matching' or 'fitting' the necessary requirements for entry into coveted educational opportunities, subtly blanketed under the discourse of meritocracy.

> This is a particularly insidious argument: it implies that those who do not succeed – even entire groups of people – are themselves responsible for any disadvantages they suffer. It discounts institutional and structural impediments to success, and ignores the fact that those who do 'succeed' in a meritocracy take steps to ensure that their children become embedded in structures that will ensure that they succeed regardless of 'merit'. (Ross, Op. Cit.)

Of course, individual motivation and achievement cannot be disregarded. Many members of disadvantaged groups can and do have high achievement levels within the education system. Within the nested hierarchies of complexity in a system, the roles and agency of individuals in the nonlinear interconnected systems implies some measure of self-determination. The position taken here is that identity, which is often signalled by membership to a group, tends to be fluid, cross-cultural and cross-social. However, while individual identity is seen as dynamic and changeable and contingent upon social construct, the very fact that identities are part of a social construct implies that there are parameters within which these constructs are confined, including the social discourse of others (teachers, peers, administrators, parents, caretakers, television actors, news commentators, etc.) who will contribute to identity of individuals. It is not possible to focus on individual construction of identity here; therefore this chapter will look at how the dialogic interaction of 'discourse and the politics of representation' (McLaren,

2010: 196) contribute to the dilemma of targeting social inequality in education.

> [S]ocial reproduction of prevalent ideologies is not a smoothly flowing process; it is a process of constant tension, challenges and negotiation between social actors. By highlighting the 'dialogue' between policy and practice, we (…) foreground the way in which ideologised notions or categories become linked and 'naturalised' (Blommaert and Verschueren 1998) so that they become recursive 'commonsense' background to other instances of discourse. (Dooly, Vallejo and Unamuno, 2009: 6)

As we stated in our introductory chapter, 'there remains an inherent traditionalism in much educational policy, whatever the extent to which the rhetoric of transformation is employed. Education [is expected to] support and legitimise current political, social and economic norms'. The social reproduction of prevalent ideologies may help explain the failure of some remedialisation policies based on denial or impossibility of success for such programmes (see introductory chapter). Other discourse may lead to a stereotyping of diversity as the inevitable consequence of inherent factors (ethnicity, economic power, ability, etc.) and efforts for remedialisation of disadvantages may even cause disadvantaged groups to be blamed for lack of success.

Agentive links between diversity and inequity

Individual activities can affect the larger society. For instance, individual activities following the identification of minority, disadvantaged groups may have an effect on school populations. Once specific groups have been identified as being in need of remediation, the 'achieving' majority may perceive this group as underachieving, and their presence as a threat to the standards achieved by members of other groups. This, in turn, can lead to segregation, isolation, and potential stereotyping.

This is corroborated by studies carried out in the United States which suggest that, despite government attempts to promote integration of minorities in public schools, levels of school segregation are still very high (Reardon, Yun, and Eitle, 2000). Furthermore, studies demonstrate that segregation in the schools contributes to academic achievement gaps between different groups (Cardand Rothstein, 2007; Mickelson, 2001). Some studies attribute at least part of the problem with so-called patterns of 'white flight' as disadvantaged groups are left in underperforming schools while majority groups begin to move to other schools. This may reinforce the 'achieving' majority's biased assumptions about school quality (for instance a wrongly conceived notion that a high percentage of minority student profile in the school will result in the need for teachers and schools to divert more resources towards helping 'under prepared' students and ignoring other students). In studies of large cities in the USA, it has been demonstrated that when parents choose to send their children to alternative schools, the neighbourhood schools became more segregated (Fairlie and Resch, 2002; Sohoni and Saporito, 2009). Renzulli and Evans (2005) found that in situations where there are more alternative school options in the neighbourhood (particularly charter schools) there were higher levels of school segregation.

In a 1990s study of the state of Louisiana (USA), Bankston and Caldas (2000) found private school enrolment to be higher in districts where there were more minority students. In this way, cultural and social perceptions become intertwined with perceptions of academic quality. Along these lines, Zhang (2008) found that educational attainment levels of neighbourhood schools and subsequent perceptions of academic quality were associated with higher rates of public school enrolment for majority group students. At the same time the author found that the higher the percentage of minority students the more negative perception of academic quality. Within the complexity theory, this can be understood as individuals acting on information (even if it is unsubstantiated information) about the social systems and their environments (Marion, 1999). If parents consider the percentage of minority group enrolment in a school as an indicator of school quality they may opt for alternative schooling for their children. This symbolic and physical devaluation of the schools then feed into already existent stereotypes as students who are unable to meet the economic demands of optional education opportunities are left within less resourced public schools. According to Leithwood and Fullan (2003)

> Histories of poor school performance for such students may result from neglect on behalf of the school and/or district leaders, allocation of the least able teachers and most limited resources to the most needy schools and students, low expectations, or lack of knowledge of effective strategies for working with particular kinds of students in challenging contexts. (p.13)

This 'agentive link' between perceptions and values (undervaluing a school with minority population) demonstrates the nested hierarchies of 'structures of communication, systems of meaning, or discourse, ideologies, roles of individuals (…), power relations, values, individual perceptions, technology, knowledge, configurations of energy, matter, money, information fluxes, human time allocation structures, rituals, and others' (Manuel-Navarette (nd.): 12). Similarly, the naturalised 'systems of meaning' become part of particular social domains, including education and knowledge production (McLaren, 2010). As Leithwood and Fullan (2003) point out, poor school performance –especially in schools with a large percentage of disadvantaged groups– is often the result of poorer access to 'knowledge production' through less experienced, less prepared teachers, adapted and less challenging curricula, and fewer school resources.

The school curriculum plays a key role in access to educational opportunities as well as outcome (Dooly, Vallejo and Unamuno, 2009; see also the discussion on subject balance and other structural issues in chapter three). Jenks (2005) sees the school curriculum as a principal unit of analysis, which contingently with school as a social space, gives meaning to the formal organization of the school experience as a social and socialising process. For Jenks, the curriculum is a spatial concept and has a strategic role in 'mapping out the whole in-school experience of the child through a combination of space, time, location, content, proximity, isolation, insulation, integration and hierarchy' (Jenks, 2005: 76). Schools – as physical spaces and social spaces – make up the spatial theories of cognitive and bodily development deemed necessary for the students inside the school walls. The power relations inside the school, the embedded and explicit values promoted or ignored, the resources, the configurations of technological, physical and human time allocation structures, routines ... all of these configurations make up the nested hierarchies of the complex educational system.

The 'social space' inside schools that have become highly segregated and which are widely perceived as having lower academic quality may have a negative socialising effect on the students and teachers themselves due to the dynamics of the embedded values, power structures, and social interactions of everyone involved. The curriculum may become less challenging due to lowered expectations, resources may be diverted, and teachers and pupils may become less motivated, to name a few possibilities. Of course, each situation is a case unto itself, however, from a macro-perspective, teasing out moments of path dependency of different variables and contingent turning points of nested hierarchies can provide more insight into different kinds of socially structured inequality such as those described above.

Intersubjective links between diversity and inequity

As we have seen, the inherently nonlinear interconnected systems that can
lead to inequity in education may be discursive, agentive, individual,
collective, micro or macro or all of these. Focusing on the schools as
social spaces underscores the interaction and intersubjectivity of everyone
involved in the school at all levels of hierarchy. Intersubjectivity can be
understood as the manifestation of shared meanings constructed by people
in their interactions with each other. Lindblom and Ziemke (2008) suggest
that intersubjectivity is the cradle of social interaction and cognition.
Along similar lines, recent research explores how one of the core
formative principles for identity lies, not in social relations, but rather
relationality (or what Holloway, 2010, refers to as 'unconscious
intersubjective dynamics'). In her research, Holloway underscores the
importance of context, affective states, socially constructed meaning,
agency, and the complexity of personal experience in the construction of
shared knowledge.

Understanding intersubjectivity and shared meaning as a type of popular
consciousness, via 'common sense.' (Dooly, 2009) helps provide insight
into how individuals may affect meaning within dynamic systems
(Hardman, 2010). This also helps explain why it has been shown that
'naturalised' discourse has routinely 'problematised' students from
minority groups. For instance, Grosvenor (1989) describes how children
from minority ethnic groups were discursively identified as 'problems' to
be dealt with in post-World War II years in the UK. In a more recent
study, Dooly (2009) describes how linguistically and culturally diverse
classes were recurrently identified as 'problematic', 'difficult', or 'hard' to
teach by teachers of different ages, nationalities, disciplines and
backgrounds. 'Problematised' students may be linked to the 'inequality
markers' identified in chapter three, especially in school and social
exclusion.

Individuals and collectivities reproduce themselves both biologically and
culturally, in part through 'naturalised' discourse; children are 'imbued
with social values and cultural capital through early socialization and
formal education' (Jenks, 2005: 90). Intersubjectively, then, groups that
have been identified as needing remediation may consequently have
lowered expectations of themselves. Rist (2000) found significant
differences in the dynamics of interaction between teachers and students of
diverse backgrounds, furthering the impact of oppression and unfair

education for these students. Rist found that teachers hold an approximate notion of the 'ideal type' student who will be successful in school and society and that this image provides a measure for them to form an opinion of all students. Pupils who do not fit within the parameters of the ideal type are treated as failures without the opportunity to prove themselves. The intersubjectivity between teacher and pupil implies that constructed meanings are made manifest in human interactions (Lindblom and Ziemke, 2008) thus helping bringing about the 'self-fulfilling prophecy' (see chapter six). Students who are expected to do well, tend to do well. Those who are expected to fail, often do so.

Furthermore, efforts to empower students from disadvantaged groups, to involve them in the solutions, may lead to them being blamed for lack of success, if the remediation does not achieve the desired outcomes. After all, empowerment entails gaining ground within an already established system. Thus, if solutions are provided that are meant to empower and the solutions fall short this implies failure on part of the individual, not the system. This, in turn, may reinforce lowered self-expectations as well as buttressing assumed traits and low expectations of the disadvantaged group, as viewed by others.

In addition, if empowerment is to come from within the system, the individual must first believe in that system. Ogbu (1992) developed the theory that minority groups were unlikely to believe schooling credentials could provide a means of 'upward mobility' just as Willis found that school success was not important for the working class 'lads' in his study because they realised their destinies were in blue collar labour that did not require academic training (quoted in Garnett, 2010: 109).

> Students from oppressed groups may be sceptical of the rewards offered
> by schooling credentials; teachers may – even subconsciously – doubt the
> aptitude of the same students. (Garnett, 2010: 109)

Following on Ogbu, Cummins (1998, 2000) hypothesised that broader social power relations (e.g. media representations of minorities produced by dominant groups) merge into education, particularly in teacher perceptions of students and this 'naturalised' discourse can lead to educational inequality. The 'emergence' of constructed understandings of students' assumed traits and proficiency, along with the complicit nature of the persons involved dynamically affect the system (Davis and Sumara, 2006); in other words, the classroom relationships, the dis/empowerment of students based on fallacious assumptions will affect the classroom dynamic in various ways, including the ignoring or devaluing of competences not associated with mainstream education. Armandaiz (2001) found that minority students' skills, knowledge, and self-concepts were consistently and systematically devalued by mainstream teachers.

Low expectations may extend to parental involvement and support. While teachers may invest time and provide learning support for disadvantaged students, at the same time they may assume that parental support will be negligible and therefore what goes on inside the classroom will stop at the classroom door. Research shows, however, that parents of students from disadvantaged groups are usually concerned and involved (although they may not have resources to provide adequate support). The National Centre for Education Statistics found that parents of low-income students have less opportunities and access for school involvement due to multiple jobs, lack of transportation or expensive childcare (2005), implying that it is not parental failure but rather institutional failure to accommodate to low-income family timetables and needs. Other research indicates that low-income parents hold similar attitudes to wealthy parents about education, and are as concerned for their children's education (Compton-Lilly, 2003; Lareau and Horvat, 1999).

Collective and individual identities exist and impact on one another reciprocally. In this sense, there is a continuous construction of self and identity (and identity of other), both explicitly and through a background of implicit 'worldly' meanings (Bourdieu, 1993) or 'background of commonsense knowledge'. Reflexive processes can accelerate or relativise these identities, creating socially constructed shared meanings that may lead to problems within the very policies that identify underachieving groups –in this case, a commonly held assumption that underachieving groups do not have the proper infrastructure and support outside of the classroom.

Final words

Reconciling the concept of individual agency with the idea that social structures have causal powers is a well known dilemma in social science (Banfield, 2010). At the same time, it is important to be able to theorise about the intersectionality of multiple complex social inequalities (Walby, 2007) in order to better understand 'the ontological depth of each set of social relations' (p. 454). Bhaskar (1998) proposes that there is an analytic dualism between structure and agency; 'an ontological hiatus between society and people' (p. 37). 'Both structures and agents have distinct causal powers and effectivities: each are emergently real' (Banfield, 2010: 136). Using Bhaskar's theory as a starting point, Banfield argues that 'individuals' and 'structures' are 'ontologically (and analytically) distinguishable and stratified. In other words, societies (which pre-exist people) are not agents and people (who make societies) are not social structures' (ibid.).

However, this stratification implies relationships between generative mechanisms and that they cannot be reduced to simple horizontal correspondence (e.g. top-down determinism or exaggerated individual agency). 'Higher-level mechanisms are rooted in lower ones: existing by virtue of, but not reducible to them' (Banfield, 2010:137). Because the stratification is emergent (contingent upon multiple sets of social relationships and intersecting pathways of events occurring across various nested hierarchies or domains), the possibility of 'horizontal engagement with other co-determining mechanisms' means that

> certain powers may be nullified and others amplified. How powers actually play out in different contexts and at other times is a matter for empirical work. There are no pre-determined guarantees. (Banfield, 2010:148)

This book is written from the viewpoint that just because there are no 'pre-determined guarantees', this does not mean that educational inequity should be accepted as an inevitable outcome of society. As stated in the introduction, it is our position that that educational stakeholders (as agents with causal powers) need to reconceptualise what is meant by inequality and reformulate their characterisations and explanations of why some groups do not achieve educationally as well as others. Programmes (as part of the social structure with causal power) need to be redesigned to address inequity towards the population as a whole, rather than to isolate on particular communities, especially considering that programmes aimed only at specific populations may carry its own discursive link to 'naturalised ideology' that can be harmful to that same group.

CHAPTER SIX

TALKING TO THE MAJORITY

So far we have largely explored why attempts to address inequalities in education have not succeeded. We now turn to use this analysis to consider what might be the possible ways in which policies might be directed towards ensuring more equitable outcomes. We have shown that the causes of failure (of policies and of educational attainments) have complex origins, and the ways forward are, unsurprisingly, just as multifaceted and intricate. And, just as the causes of educational inequity and failure are interlinked and feed on each other, so will the solutions be entangled and attached to each other: this will not be a shopping list from which some items might be selected as more appealing (or cheaper) and others discarded – it is presented as a package, in which all elements are important.

We have emphasised that we have been concerned specifically with inequalities in education that are attached to particular groups or categories, rather than about individual differences. Our analysis has therefore related educational and social inequalities to social structures, rather than to personal attributes. Nevertheless, decisions about the level of educational engagement, and the extent to which the individual elects to attempt the next level of education are, in part, the consequence of individual actions. Some of these actions will be taken by those responsible for the application of educational policy, such as making decisions on which type of education particular individuals might take – whether this be streaming pupils towards particular subjects, examinations, or types of schooling, or offering advice to pupils about available options. Other factors will be governed by actions taken by the individual pupil (or their families).

Archer and Hutchings (2000) investigated the decisions made by working-class young people on whether to enter further and higher education, in which the desire to potentially 'better one's self' was balanced against factors such as a history of educational non-success, fear of failure, and the potential costs of such a decision. The decisions that are made will tend to be risk-averse, but they will very often be rationalised into a discourse about further study 'not being for people like me' (see also Archer, Hutchings and Ross, 2003). Breen and Goldthorpe (1997) argued that young people used a technique of 'relative risk aversion': that their principal goal in schooling was to acquire a level of education that would allow them to attain a class position at least of the same level as that of their family, or to avoid downward mobility, but that to go beyond this in terms of studying was a matter of calculation, balancing such factors as the potential break with one's family culture implicit in moving into higher education against the risks of failure, deferring earning, accumulating debt, etc. Breen (2001) subsequently extended this to argue that two factors contributed to educational careers – pre-established family decisions about attaining a particular educational threshold and beliefs about the probability of educational success.

This analysis does not shift the sole responsibility for decision-making to the individual, because the context in which an individual, student, or their family, makes a decision about an educational threshold, or about the limit of their aspiration, or about the relative chances of success, are all conditioned by the educational discourse into which they have been encultured. Because discrete groups are responding in ways that are significantly different from the majority population, it can be suggested that these groups are systematically being regarded by educational policy-makers and professionals as being less likely to succeed, and less likely to aspire to higher levels of education or employment. They will be undertaking significantly greater risks if they attempt educational activities that are regarded as the norm by their peers in the majority population. If members of a particular group are consistently streamed into particular kinds of subjects or schooling (for example, 'non-academic' or vocational, or non-scientific), then the degree of choice that they are able to exercise later in their educational career will be curtailed. If they are persistently regarded as not likely to achieve, or are guided towards stereotypical training pathways or careers, then their aspirations will be limited. If they are expected not to be educationally successful, then they will be less likely to achieve, and if they consequently have a record of educational failure, then they are less likely to want to risk moving into contexts in which they may again fail educationally. This is not to deny agency to individuals, but to recognise that there are powerful structural and cultural constraints that limit this agency.

The discussion above has been focused on one particular example of decision-making about educational engagement: whether or not to attempt post-compulsory education. But very similar balances of risk surround decisions about educational involvement and commitment at earlier stages of an individual's schooling. The decisions about engagement with pre-schooling and levels of support for the child during compulsory schooling are made within a nexus of social engagement with educational providers, and involve calculations not merely about what time and other support can be provided within the constraints of family circumstance, but a set of expectations about the kind of reception that the educational providers might give to those of their social standing, and about what expectations there might be that any investment would have an appreciable dividend.

Nicaise (2000) has analysed these perceptions of educational attainment, and has suggested that inequalities in education can be seen as arising from two different forms of failure. Firstly, there are failures on the demand side, where unequal opportunities are the result of those 'getting the education' (pupils and their parents) 'fail' to demand adequate and appropriate educational provision. Why do they not do so? For a multitude of reasons: an expectation that if provided, it would still lead to failure; a fear of rejection and alienation because of how they anticipate their class, ethnic or other origins to be received by the educational establishments, or because of the socio-economic characteristics of social groups (such as poverty, material or cultural deprivation, health or lack of social or cultural capital). For all these reasons (identified in part by Breen (2001) above) individuals and families from these groups decline to take up educational opportunities.

Nicaise's secondly set of failures are on the supply side, where educational policies and practices lead to the disadvantageous treatment of members of a group in the educational process: this would include both institutional prejudice against these groups and the inability of institutions to actively respond to the specific and different needs of particular groups.

Both of these are structural failings; and each interacts with the other. If the 'supply side' institutions cannot adequately support the group, then they create a situation in which members of the group lower their aspirations and expectations of success, and make fewer demands on the educational system. This interaction creates the conditions for self-sustaining failure, and there seems little value in debating the primacy of either side in terms of causation. The circle needs to be broken.

Supply factors and demand factors

There is a growing body of research that demonstrated that the very existence of inequality has an impact on attainment. If learners are told, or believe, that they have some innate characteristic that suggests they may not succeed at a task, they will behave and perform less well than if they believe that they will succeed.

One of the earliest and best-known examples of the effects of discrimination on behaviour was the 'Eye of the storm' experiment conducted by the Iowa school teacher Jane Elliott in 1968. She organised her class of 8 – 9 year olds into a brown-eyed and a blue-eyed group. The blue-eyed group were told that they were superior, justified by some pseudo-scientific explanations, and were give particular small privileges – five minutes extra playtime, second helpings at lunch, sitting at the front of the class – and were encouraged to keep separate from the brown-eyed children. She reported that very quickly changes in behaviour: the blue-eyed children became arrogant, and were unpleasant to the less privileged group, and the brown-eyed children became timid and subservient, and their educational attainment was affected. All this occurred in a single day: the exercise was reversed the next day. After this, the children were debriefed, and discussed their feelings about the exercise, which had been prompted by their negative remarks about Black Americans following the assassination of Martin Luther King. This became the basis of a series of programmes to raise awareness of discrimination and its effects (Peters, 1971, 1987). The experiment itself has been widely criticised as unethical (eg Goodson and Sikes 2001; Sikes, 2008).

Steele and Aronson (1995) report a more rigorous experiment, in which the standardised Graduate Record Examination for graduate school entrants was given to two groups of students: one was told that it was a test of their ability; the second were explicitly told that it did not measure ability, but was given for other diagnostic purposes.

While White students performed equally well under both conditions, the Black students performed significantly less well when they were under the impression that they were being measured. The difference (figure 6.1) they called the 'Stereotype Threat'.

Figure 6.1: The Stereotype Threat

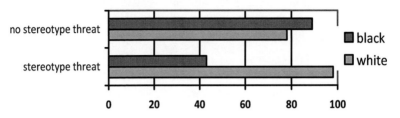

Source: based on Aronson, J., Steele, C., Salinas, M, and Lustina, M. (1998) The Effects of Stereotype Threat on the Standardised Test Performance of College Students, in Aronson (ed) *Readings About the Social Animal*, NY: Freeman 1998

A third example, the most recent, is from India. Hoff and Pandey (2004) set a maze-solving task to groups of 11 and 12 year old boys that contained equal numbers of low caste and high caste members. They were asked to solve the mazes without initially being aware of each other's caste origins. The low caste boys did very slightly better than the high caste boys. The experimenters then read out a list of the names of the boys, the villages each lived in, fathers' names, grandfathers' names and caste: each boy had to confirm these details were correct to the group. The maze solving patterns were then resumed, and the performance of the low caste boys fell sharply (Figure 6.2).

Figure 6.2: Average performance by low caste and high caste

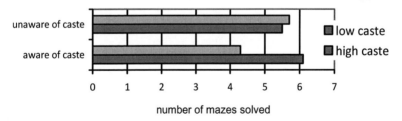

number of mazes solved

Source: based on Figure 4. Average performance by low caste and high caste in Piece Rate and Random Winner treatments: Average number of mazes solved, Round 2, Karla Hoff, K. and Pandey, P. (2004)

These three examples show that if a learner is conscious of their socially-disadvantaged status, their performance, and their expectation of performance, will be lessened. In most educational settings, those responsible for educational provision also have different expectations of how different groups will perform, and will make decisions about what outcomes to expect based on the students gender, ethnic origin, social class – or whatever distinguishing characteristic they believe may impact on attainment and potential.

A recent study by Strand (2012: in press) illustrates this. In the English system of public examination at age 14, all students are entered for national Standard Assessment Tests in (among other subjects) Mathematics and Science. Because there is in these subjects an inevitably very wide range of ability to test, the tests are tiered: teachers decide which of one of two tiers in science, and which of four tiers in mathematics, each student will take. Each tier gives access to a limited range of outcomes with the highest test outcomes achievable only if students are entered by their teachers to the higher tiers. Thus in science, the two tiers are a lower tier 3-6 and a higher tier 5-7, where each tier has different papers targeted at a restricted set of levels. The lower tier primarily to rate students at levels 4 and 5, and the higher tier to rate pupils at 6. But the highest level, 7, can only be awarded to students who take the higher tier paper. But there is a risk entering the higher tier paper: if the student fails to get level 5, there is only a very narrow range of marks that can lead to a compensatory level 4, otherwise the student is not awarded a level and is graded 'unclassified' - a very undesirable result. In mathematics, the four levels make the system more complex. The decision as to which tier a student is entered for is down to the teacher's professional judgment, based on their perceptions of how each student can cope with the content and structure of the test.

There had been a number of studies that suggested that minority ethnic students were less likely to be entered by their teachers to the higher test tiers, and so were not able to achieve the highest test outcomes, but these were studies of schools that were selected because their Black students were performing below the average for all pupils at age 14, and they were not a representative sample (Gillborn and Youdell, 2000; Tikly, Haynes, Caballero and Hill, 2006). So the suspicion that teachers were systematically entering Black students for lower tier examinations because of their lower expectations remained a suspicion: it could have been that these expectations were well grounded for each individual concerned, rather than a more general presumption based on ethnicity.

Strand had access to a much larger data set, based on the Longitudinal Study of Young People in England, which was random, national, and included data based in interviews with students and their parents (on such parental aspirations, family structure, parents' own educational achievements, computer access, etc), as well as standard data on prior attainment in these subjects at age 11, socio-economic background, special educational needs, school attendance patterns, and so on. From this, he was able to create prior attainment models and family background models, and use this to see whether gender, ethnicity, socio-economic status helped explain teacher decisions about which tier of examination Black pupils were entered for. Overall, he found 'that for every three White British students entered for the higher tier only two Black Caribbean students of the same prior attainment are entered' (p 10). This was not a reflection of their lower prior attainment: 'Black Caribbean students are under-represented relative to White British students with the same prior age 11 test scores. Neither is it explained by differences in gender, social class of the home, maternal education, socio-economic deprivation, home ownership or single parent households' (14).

This complements and extends many earlier studies, which were more limited in their scope, or were more ethnographic in their nature. Bennett *et al.* (1993) found that teachers' academic judgements were strongly influenced by their view of students' behaviour: if the teacher thought that a student's behaviour was 'bad' in some way, then the student was judged to be poorer academically. Students of Black Caribbean are not infrequently judged to present challenging behaviour, and more teachers report problematic behaviour from this group than from students of other ethnic backgrounds (Mortimore *et al.*, 1988). Other studies based on school ethnographies suggest that behavioural criteria, not just cognitive results, are used when students are allocated to examination sets and streams, to the particular disadvantage of Black students (Gillborn, 1990; Gillborn and Youdell, 2000; Rollock, 2007).

The consequence of such educational practice is, of course, to depress the mean educational attainment level of this group of students, since the higher rankings are unattainable from the tiers that they are entered for. This, as will now be evident, has two consequences: firstly, it confirms the teachers in their behaviour. Black students do have lower test results than other students, and it therefore seems appropriate to protect them from the risk of an unclassified score by entering them from a test that will at least safely give them a 4 grade. The prejudice may be unwitting, or it may be taken for what are thought the student's best interests. The second consequence is, in a way, even more insidious: Black students themselves, seeing these results, will begin to assume that they are innately inferior in these subjects, and then – *pace* the Eye of the Storm, Steele and Aronson (1995), Hoff and Pandey (2004), above - actually perform worse. This is more than a self-fulfilling prophecy.

The evidence summarised above around Black students can be extended to other social groups. For example, around social class, Stephen Ball, Dianne Reay and others have shown systematic educational disadvantages in schools in the UK: Ball (2003) tracks middle class strategies to ensure their children 'succeed', and Reay (2004) and Reay *et al.* (2005) examine class advantage and disadvantage in a range of school settings. Archer, Ross and Hutchings (2003) look at issues around higher education and social class. In the United States, Rist (2000 described how state schools mirror the class system and are actively involved in maintaining it. He analysed observations of a ghetto class over three years of early education, showing how the teacher organised reading groups which reflected the social class composition. Teacher behaviour toward the different social classes was a significant influence on the children's achievement.

Expectations matter. Students and parents' expectations are important, because these not only affect the actual results achieved (while high expectations lead to high results, and low expectations lead to low results in not a total explanation, it is a very important contributory factor), but can also lead to a decreased expectation from parents and pupils for educational attention and resources. Given the competition for these, lower expectations and demands will often mean that those with competing and more vocal demands will get more. Teacher and educationalist expectations are important, because these critically impinge on the educational responses of the students and their learning attainment. The two interact: each causes the other (Local Government Association, 2008).

Two precursors

But before examining how these two sets of expectations can be raised and managed, there are two important preparatory activities that need to be tackled.

Collecting accurate and comprehensive data

It is critical first to have accurate data about the attainment of all the various groups (and intersections of groups), and the social and demographic backgrounds of students, and to have these on an individual basis, so that statistical monitoring can be carried out. This, of course, raises issues about confidentiality, labelling, and data security that must be addressed. It also requires generating the confidence of the population that gathering band recording such data is necessary, useful, and that it will be employed for proper and legitimate purposes.

These purposes are threefold. First, it is necessary to determine whether inequalities exist for a particular group, and to estimate their independence of other factors. It's necessary to know what the distinguishing variables, or concatenation of variables is, and the degree of under-attainment. This allows a decision to be made about whether there is an issue, and if action is needed. It also allows some mapping of the extent of the problem: is this group located in particular areas of concentration, or dispersed? Does the level of inequity appear to vary according to such dispersal? What are the interactions between different variables? The second purpose is to use this data to determine what kind of action is necessary. Should resources be targeted in a particular way: to particular children, families, schools or locations? Or should they be used more broadly? Does the data suggest policies are directed at particular age groups or stages of education; or at particular curricular areas? Thirdly, such data collection allows the effective monitoring of any intervention. Policies need to be effective, and without reliable and consistent data, it is impossible to know whether particular interventions are effective or not, whether modifications are needed, or other targets should be identified.

This may sound straightforward, but there are many potential complications. Identifying particular at-risk groups depends on matters of definition, and often of self-identification. In the UK, 'Black' was regarded as an adequate ethnic group identifier in the 1960s (when the predominant Black school population was of Caribbean origin). In the 1980s, 'Black African' and 'Black Caribbean' were differentiated, as it was thought that there was some variation between the two groups; by the late 1990s, 'West African' and 'East African' became significant, and since then particular national groups – Somali, Ghanaian, Liberian, etc have been used in particular areas, where this has seemed to allow better targeting of provision. This may not be adequate: it is inappropriate to categorise Kurds who have migrated to Europe from Turkey as 'Turkish', for example. The later is also seen (by many Kurds) as offensive – and by (some Turks) as politically accurate and necessary: this is an added level of complication when defining groups. As Mannitz (2004b) observed in a comparison of educational policies in Britain, Germany, France and the Netherlands,

> The co-existence of disparate cultures that is entailed in the construction of Britishness ... is part of the dominant rhetoric that minority pupils in London adopted with their articulation of multiple identities. ... This ... points to problems that stem from the dominant model of the multicultural society, namely segmentary boundary effects of the concept of a social mosaic, in interaction with a heightened awareness of anti-discrimination that relies on individuals being perceived as group members. (p 297)

Given the multiplicity of identities that an individual may express, with different identities being declared contingently (both spatially and temporarily), which subjectivities should be identified for analysis of potential educational inequity? Who should be asked to declare such affiliations, community, parent or child? Given the potential impermanence and very subjectivity of such labels, what issues are there in terms of reliability and consistency over time? These are difficult, but not insurmountable issues. The problem does not only relate to issues of ethnic identity, but also to other potential areas of discrimination, resource allocation and inequity. For example, such condition as Attention-Deficit Hyperactivity Syndrome (ADHS), there are clearly issues of levels of (parental and school) seeking of diagnoses, and of the criteria for diagnoses, as the US Federal agency the Centre for Disease Control and Prevention has identified in mapping the incidence of ADHS diagnosis (Figure 6.3).

It is improbable that there are variations between the different states – in social, environmental or genetic factors – that explain these differences: there is probably some variations in local expectations of the prevalence – even the existence – of such a syndrome.

Figure 6.3: Variation in incidence of diagnosis of Attention-Deficit Hyperactivity Syndrome in the United States, on a State-by-State basis, 2007-2008

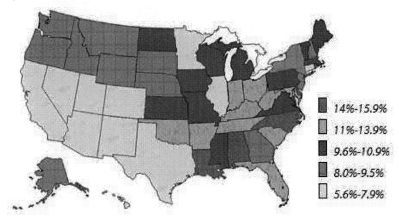

14%-15.9%

11%-13.9%

9.6%-10.9%

8.0%-9.5%

5.6%-7.9%

Source: US Center for Disease Control and Prevention, Atlanta GA
http://www.cdc.gov/ncbddd/adhd/data.html

Monitor progress and evaluating interventions

When we were conducting the EPASI study for the European Commission, which led us to write this book (see page 16), we analysed over 280 different intervention projects in 14 different European countries. All were explicitly designed to tackle inequities in education, and they were predominantly undertaken by national and local educational agencies and institutions (a few by non-governmental agencies and charitable foundations). What we found particularly remarkable was that very few of them were evaluated in terms of their effectiveness, and most of those that were appeared not to have been subject to any rigorous examination. Such assessments that were made were initiated well after the programme began, or lacked a reasonable understanding of the base position, or had no control group, or were carried out by the intervention agency itself. These evaluations were almost always positive and unreflective. Curiously, most of those interventions that were evaluated positively were not then adopted as normal mainstream practice. The overall impression was of piecemeal intervention, in which funders appeared to lose interest after the projects were initiated. For example, in Sweden, the (former) National Agency of School Improvement report that evaluations are seldom budgeted (Hartsmar 2008). This may be an unduly cynical interpretation, but it may not always be in a funding agency's interest to have an objective assessment of the projects it initiates.

We suggest it is essential that when interventions are planned there should be a concomitant commitment to an independent evaluation, which starts alongside the intervention programme itself, continues after the intervention is completed, that looks where possible at control groups, and which maintains a proper distance from those providing the evaluation, in order to maintain their objectivity. This will inevitably be an additional expense – perhaps between 5% and 15% of the cost of the project – but it is essential if a government is to know that the objectives have been achieved. There should be a parallel understanding that if an intervention is found to be successful then funding ought to be available to 'mainstream' the programme: it is imprudent to test out and evaluate interventions that are so expensive that they cannot be implemented to address the needs of a whole population.

Address issues of demand

How can policies address demands made by groups and communities that fail to achieve educationally, and are thus further disadvantaged and subject to more inequities? This is as critical as addressing supply-side issues: communities, parents, and above all students themselves need to have confidence in their abilities to succeed, and to be able to articulate these expectations, and to expect and require educational authorities to meet them. In the competitive social environment associated with liberal social market economies and meritocratic societies, the demands of the privileged (largely middle-class) achievers for educational resources will inevitably be an insistent clamour, sometimes shrill (Ball, 2003). Disadvantaged groups need to be empowered to be at least as much as these groups to insist that their children are also given the specific educational resources and programmes that they need in order to achieve equality of outcome.

Communities and parents need to be encouraged and supported to be involved in the planning and delivery of educational programmes and practices. This means sensitively and carefully working with existing community organisations, to help them articulate needs and concerns in ways that will convince both planners and the wider community that needs, programmes and resources are justly and legitimately needed for specifically deprived communities. Equally, such inclusion in planning processes must be used to ensure that programmes are devised with due sensitivity for cultural and social differences, recognising that programmes must be constructed around a group, rather than simply tailored to adjust to them. Whilst ideally in any democracy members of different communities will be part of the regular local and national governmental bodies and processes, it cannot simply be assumed that the usual civil participation processes will produce a fully representative mix, and it may be necessary to ensure that there are additional participatory processes available for new or unrepresented minorities: the educational disadvantage they experience will not work to their advantage in the democratic process.

Groups, communities, parents all need to be involved at all levels in educational management, processes and provision, for a variety of reasons, which together ensure the full articulation of demand and expectation of equity. Involving communities in decision making, and expecting communities to share responsibility in the implementation and evaluation of programmes that aim at educational equity is an intrinsic part of the raising of expectations of success: under-performing groups are not the authors of their own misfortune, but are the key actors who will achieve the reversal of this (Local Government Association, 2008).

At the individual family unit level, parents and pupils also need to have high expectations. Many under-achieving groups may already have this – typically, new migrants very often have high ambitions for their children, and expect success: the drive to better themselves is often an important element in the decision to migrate. But this is not true of all minorities and under-achieving groups: for many, there have been generations of educational failure, and the inculcation of a culture of not doing well at school. Education becomes seen as 'not for helices of us', an attitude that is compounded by the exigencies of relative poverty and having little time (or experience) of helping their children to achieve in school.

Specific programmes directed at the parents of young children can provide strategies for effective parental support for learning, raising awareness of the importance of the home environment in encouraging learning and in expecting educational attainments.

In parallel to this empowering of communities, parents and students is the separate task of educating the majority population about the needs and rights of minorities in a diverse and unequal society. They too must have expectations of the educational success that will be achieved by hitherto disadvantaged and underachieving groups. Much of the discrimination against underachieving groups – whether those with disabilities, those of working class background, or from minority ethnic or linguistic groups – is in part supported by beliefs in the ineducability of members of these groups. This is used to justify inequalities, but also generates a climate of low expectations of members of these groups. This critically pervades all aspects of society, and often contributes to the low expectations of success held within the minority groups. The majority group members do not expect success, and are likely to discriminate against minority group members in a wide variety of ways that all help keep the minority subordinate.

Addressing issues of supply

The second major strand in any strategy to achieve educational equality lies in ensuring that educators – both the teachers and the educational establishment of policy makers and administrators – have the ability to provide the educational processes that will raise achievement, and have the expectation that all groups will succeed equally well. Teachers and other educational professionals need explicit education that addresses the understanding of diversity, and that examines and demonstrates the effect of having low expectations of particular groups of students. Teachers rarely encounter – either in their pre-service education, or in their professional updating while in service – training that deals with the education of linguistic and ethnic minorities, those who are socio-economically deprived, those with special educational needs. These are generally treated as areas of specialisation, as optional training programmes, to be taken specifically by teachers who work in particular areas where the concentration of such pupils is particularly high. This has the effect of othering these groups: they become to be seen as part of the spectrum of educational problems and issues, and thus enhance the ethos of expectations of low attainment. Teachers who elect to specialise in the teaching of these groups of children are essentially ghettoised into the outposts of the profession.

What is needed, we suggest, is to ensure that all teachers, of all students in all areas, are given specific and explicit training in understanding cultural and other diversities, on the effects of teachers having low expectations of success (and how this becomes a self-fulfilling process), and of specific ways of raining expectations and of raising educational performance. This will include understating that the language competencies of underperforming groups will need specific and sometimes additional assistance in the development of academic language competencies, and not merely of communicative competencies. It will include not only the understanding of the potential effects of their own lowered expectations of success, but also of the effects of pupils having low expectations. These competencies are needed by all teachers, in all schools and in higher education, not merely by teachers in particular areas and particular areas of specialisation, because these attitudes need to be conveyed to all students, of whatever background. These provisions for teachers should obviously be included in pre-service education, but issues of underachievement and educational inequality will not be addressed as quickly as they need to be if everything is left to the next cohort of teachers who join the profession: there need also to be support programmes for the teachers who are already in post.

Another, and complementary strand, will be to recruit teachers who come from groups that traditionally underachieve and that sufferer educational inequities – from working class backgrounds, from indigenous minority groups such as the Roma, from linguistic and ethnic minorities, and from those of migrant backgrounds.

Why should the teaching profession be more representative of disadvantaged groups in a given society? We do not expect all professions (or all other workforce groups) to represent the educationally underperforming minorities in the population. Most European countries have anti-discriminatory legislation and recruitment policies on training and appointments: but if these are followed, and the teaching profession after this has a smaller proportion of teachers from traditionally educationally under achieving groups – does it matter?

There are several arguments that suggest it is important. Most of these arise from some particular characteristics of the nature of education, and of the way we organise learning in our schools (Ross, 2002).

- Learning is a formative activity conducted through a variety of processes, some of which are explicit and very visible (for example, through the formal prescribed curriculum), and some of which are subtle, almost invisible and barely understood, even by practitioners. The processes of learning thus convey a wealth of meanings to young people at an impressionable and formative period in their lives: *who* conducts this process in an important part of the process.

- Learning is a social process: it takes place in the interactions between teacher and learner, and learner and learner. The people who take on the role of teacher play a critical part in determining the social relationships under which learning occurs. They are put very prominently inn a position of authority, trust and power. Who teaches is thus critical for the learning process (and is as critical in its own way as who learns). Designating a person as a teacher is not undertaken lightly by any society, and important messages – to society and parents, and above all to children - are conveyed in deciding who shall be given the accolade of teacher.
- Learning is undertaken by all children/young people. Many of our other social provisions are episodic and accidental. We do not all use the health service, for example, and the use that most of us make of it tends to be transitory and intermittent. We do not expect in our lives to experience a health service in the same way that we experience educational provision.
- Learning is conducted over a long period of time. Disregarding notions of life-long learning, it is a process that we require all our young people to undergo for a period of at least eleven years.

Making sure that the teaching force is simply 'representative' could be seen as simple tokenism - making sure that there are enough minority faces around. But these four characteristics of education make it very important as to whom we entrust to teach. Having a more representative proportion of teachers is critical because of the character, ubiquity, pervasiveness, duration and importance of teaching as a social activity. There are three specific reasons why we need more teachers from these particular minorities:

Firstly, teachers as a profession must have the capacity to reflect the full spectrum of cultural and social traditions and systems in their collective professional practice. Each individual teacher brings to her or his work a set of cultural norms and expectations. Good teachers are reflective and self-critically aware of this, but none of us can recognise all the culturally and socially determined mores that we carry. It is important the teaching profession as a whole can match the range of cultural and social varieties that our society contains. European countries have increasingly diverse populations, with a very wide range of cultures, customs, languages, disabilities, levels of wealth, faiths and beliefs. Our educational system needs to be delivered by teams of professionals who can match that range, in their explicit practice and in their subconscious behaviour and attitudes.

Both the formal and the hidden curriculum need to be managed and delivered in a way that reflects the varieties of social practice in our society, and this in turn demands that the teaching profession is drawn fully and explicitly from that range of cultures and ethnicities in our society. With such a range of teachers, we can aspire towards delivering an education that has the subtlety and the nuance to make each individual feel that her or his cultural set is acknowledged and valued, thus empowering her or him as a learner. Without such a range of teachers, this cannot even be an aspiration.

Secondly, racism and xenophobia – individual, institutional and otherwise – continue to be major issues in contemporary society. Racism in schools needs to be very explicitly and forcefully challenged – partly because this is the moment in the development of personal value systems that it can be stopped and challenged, and secondly because of its effects on both minority communities and the majority community. Minorities will be disempowered and disenfranchised as learners, with all the social and economic wastage that this implies. The majority groups will develop attitudes of intolerance and an inability to value diversity. Tackling discriminatory behaviour is important in classrooms and schools: but racism is not always explicit and obvious - or even intentional. Racism is very properly an important concern for all teachers, but some of the subtleties of racist practice and behaviour may be more obvious or more capable of recognition, by teachers who have themselves some direct experience of having suffered from racist behaviours themselves. Teachers from the majority community, however well intentioned, trained and experienced they are in anti-racist work, will still be unaware of and unable to identify and analyse much of the xenophobia, chauvinism and racism in society.

Thirdly, we need aspirational role models for our pupils, particularly pupils from under-achieving groups. We know that members of groups that underachieve in education are generally poorly represented in positions of power, authority and prestige in our society. We clearly need more police officers, social workers, accountants, politicians, senior civil servants, industrial leaders (and so on), from these groups- to work with young people from *all* groups, including the majority populations. But teachers are a particular and special category: they are the one face of civil society that every child will meet, every working day, through the whole of their formal education. It is therefore particularly critical that this 'face' of civil power be seen, visibly and explicitly, to represent all of our society. This is where such inclusiveness is essential. The presence of teachers drawn from all groups of our societies (from all the ranges of disability, from all the sexualities, from all social classes, from all ethnic minorities) will mean that firstly, all pupils – majority just as much as minority – will recognise that members of the minorities have as much power and prestige as any other citizen, and secondly, that pupils who themselves come from these minorities will recognise that they too can and should aspire to achievement, excellence, esteem and authority.

CHAPTER SEVEN

TOWARDS A CONCLUSION: THE WAY AHEAD

Issues of direction

We began this book with the questions: What do we expect education to do? What is its purpose? Various possible responses were discussed (do we want a skilled workforce, socially responsible individuals or to promote exceptional individuals to lead the rest?), each of which is not necessarily incompatible with the others: we came to no simple conclusions as to the purposes of education. Nevertheless, we did conclude that, whatever else they do, education systems should not reproduce social inequity. Our discussion did not delve into individual inequalities – understood here as an inevitable component of the statistical normal distribution of individual difference - and instead we attempt to comprehend the persistent social inequities that are experienced by particular socially-defined groups that have historically had significantly lower levels of educational achievement when compared to the mainstream population. These groups may often be very different, lacking any homogeneous features or identities that unite them – except that, when seen from the perspective of social equity, it is indisputable that there are common social inequalities which are directly related to educational policies, and that these arise despite constant attempts and initiatives designed to redress the issue. Education should not reproduce social inequalities, and should promote the elimination of differences between the profiles of attainment of different social groups.

These two questions thus have a key role in helping understand the consequences and undesirability of educational inequality, especially as they help foreground key stakeholders in the big picture: policy-makers, administrators, educational practitioners, students and parents. They also highlight many of the more blatant dichotomies and inconsistencies of beliefs that underlie systematised educational provision: education can either serve to transform society's values and traditions or can preserve and reproduce existing inequities. Others argue that, even if education's role is to transform social and cultural structures towards a more egalitarian society, the way in which the educational system is conceived and maintained implies an unequal distribution of educational resources (material and human), resulting in inherent inequity and lack of possibility for change.

Within the European Union, portrayals by the Commission and the Council of Ministers of Education as the means of creating opportunities for individuals to become literate, numerate, versed in arts, languages, technology and science are often yoked to more traditional educational policies that aim to propagate national and regional values and knowledge. Other writers suggest that these traditional 'social' and 'cultural' values are thinly veiled ideals shaped by capitalism, and that the education system is merely a means of propagating and feeding the capitalistic system and fulfilling economic needs. Theorists have also divided education as a promulgator of either cultural capita or economic capital, both being controlled by social forces within hierarchical infrastructures. Consequently schools recreate the social and economic hierarchies within which the system is embedded, 'using the processes of selection and teaching, judging and comparing performance in these activities against the *habitus* of the middle class, and thus effectively discriminating against all those students who do not have access' to such cultural capital (chapter one). Such analysis, comparing cultural capital to an economic analysis (the haves and the have-nots of socially and culturally recognised knowledge capital, for instance) allows a deeper understanding into the perpetuation of educational inequalities.

Why systems fail

We suggest, based on our analysis, that very often the intentions to address inequity run into head-on collision with other policy initiatives, or even with entrenched ideologies. We noted in the first chapter the incremental competitive focus within education (and the subsequent increase in attention to rankings and standardised testing), linked to national unease and consequent policies that aim to promote higher national rankings which will lead to supposed economic benefits. All of these are deeply embedded in this neo-liberal competitive model for research (creation of cultural capital) and education (reproduction of the same).

At the same time, it must be recognised that educational initiatives can serve as a potent engine for social change and transformation, as testified by the numerous reports, policies, projects and initiatives coming from regional, national and European commissions and organisations, many of them aimed at specific disadvantaged groups. The understanding of inequalities in this book borrows from Burchardt and Vizard's (2008) heuristic divisions: inequality of outcome; inequalities in autonomy; and inequalities in processes. Educational policies can and should address these inequalities, but we argue that the emphasis must be placed on the outcomes of these policies, not simply on their intentions.

A reconceptualisation of inequality is required. This can be achieved by reformulating the characteristics of specific groups who consistently achieve lower, educationally, than other groups as well as reformulating the reasons provided for this lower achievement. Moreover, a closer look at inequality is called for. Equality is usually understood as a condition where individuals have the same quantity of a particular good or service, or the same rank or status, or are valued the same. This implies that there may be inequality in material goods, but most individuals are on equal terms as far as rights and social conditions. However, it is argued that equal conditions do not imply equal access to all social domains. This is where the concept of equity comes into play; inequity implies that unequal distribution of a service such as education is a social injustice (Holsinger and Jacob 2009). Nevertheless, what is also critical is an explanatory understanding of why inequities arise and why they persist, because competing ideologies give rise to competing and inconsistent policy responses.

In economic terms, several contrasting perspectives have become very prominent in attempting to explain - or sometimes excuse - inequality. Liberalism (whether libertarian, classical, or neo-liberal) sees individual differences as the main reason for inequalities, and as a necessary feature of a prosperous society; because individuals have the right to possess whatever they are able to legally obtain, this promotes efficiency and risk-taking and brings greater general wealth to society as a whole. Similarly, meritocracy holds that the distribution of higher responsibility positions in the workplace, and hence of resources, should be based on an individual's merit or ability and therefore inequality is inevitable, but that wealth will be increased from generation to generation.

Marxism, on the other hand, directly links inequality to political and material infrastructures. Wealth should be (more or less) evenly distributed between all individuals of a society, based on necessity rather than individual production or efficiency. Many theorists who argue from such a perspective of social justice see inequalities as a debilitating factor for all society. For example, social inequality that creates situations of poverty lead to an increase in crime and a decrease in health in certain sectors of the population, and this then affects others, in the wealthier sectors, as they may become victims of crime and must pay, through taxation, for the taking care of the ill.

These different ideologies have led to conflicting policy arguments about the responsibility for tackling social inequality, and if so, the best way. Some might argue that elimination of poverty and improvement of education is the way to reduce social inequality and injustice while others argue that direct intervention is pointless as long as members of society lack the capability of taking advantage of the possibilities offered for social and political development, such as those that might stem from direct intervention of neo-liberal policies. What stands out particularly, in view of these differing positions, is that arguments for addressing group inequalities from the perspective of human rights is vastly different from the instrumental economic argument that inequalities are wasteful.

The book does not seek to compare economic and educational inequality. While the main thrust of Wilkinson and Pickett's (2009) argument is to suggest that the more equal the distribution of wealth in a society, the more likely for longevity for all individuals, including rich and poor, they also suggest that differences in the educational performances of individuals are affected by the overall level of inequities in the particular society in which the individuals live. The higher the level of inequality in a society, as measured by the Gini coefficient, the greater the disparity between individual educational attainments, according to background and income. In other words, a low-income student from Portugal (with a high Gini coefficient) will fare worse than a low-income student from Denmark, where there is greater equality in the distribution of income.

But even if the possibility of real equality of educational opportunity exists, the distribution of educational attainments will still be different, based on individual human diversity. Nevertheless, this should not mean that some social *groups* (as opposed to *individuals*) would have differences in educational attainments. An equivalent and comparable range of educational outcomes by all social groups should be the expected outcome: that this is not so, in the face of policies that are designed to create equality of educational opportunity, demonstrates the poverty and irrelevance of educational policies that are constructed only around equal opportunities. The existence of inequality in education is best demonstrated by considering group educational outcomes – that is through persistent lower achievement by specific social groups. In other words, in a system where there is equality in terms of educational access and treatment, the outcomes may not be equal among individuals, but when there are notable differences of attainment across a broad social group, we understand that as educational inequity: and this is the systematic and collective failure of educational providers to deliver appropriate educational services to a minority group of the population because of their social, cultural, linguistic or behavioural characteristics. Such policies and practices amount to discrimination – be it through unintentional (or intentional) prejudice, ignorance, thoughtlessness and stereotyping: a group as a whole achieves lower educational outcomes than the majority population.

In the context of the European Union, our analysis of different policies leads us to conclude that there is an increasingly instrumentalist educational agenda underlying many of the current policies and practices, with a principal focus being the employability of the upcoming generations. If there is a high number of 'unemployable' (unprepared for the demands of the current and future labour market) then these policies will contribute to equitable social structures as situations of poverty through unemployment go down. However, another underlying axis of European educational policies is on competitive educational systems – as seen in the rankings at local, national and European levels, credit-systems for access to limited, competitive higher education slots – which do contribute to educational inequity and structural inequality, leading to inevitable ambiguity and conflicts in these same policies.

As many European countries move towards the marketisation of education (e.g. Ball 2003), schooling becomes the 'coin' of preference, the commodity by which better paid employment can be obtained. This increasingly close relationship between enterprise and education also implies more normatively-referenced assessment of individuals wherein some must necessarily fail in order for others to obtain the coveted objectives of school placement, university entry, etc. This marketisation of education feeds into the 'meritocracy' explanation for persistent educational disadvantages of specific groups. This argument that the 'deserving' will inevitably 'rise' to the top and thus ensure that 'the best' individuals will be appointed to posts of responsibility is based on educational performance, placing the onus of failure upon the individuals who do not attain high levels of educational performance. Meritocracy does not take into account institutional and structural barriers to success, or the lack of access to the social and cultural capital (Bourdieu, 1993) that is embedded in the habitus of those more advantaged groups that generally succeed in educational performance.

Within the argument of meritocracy, the educational system has a principal role of assessing the individual's attainment, and thus filtering the ones who have the 'ability' to succeed from those who do not. The role of education is not to equip all individuals with the abilities, skills and understanding to become fulfilled members of society, indeed, in order for some to succeed, others must necessarily fail – thus creating institutionalised and codified (and 'rationalised') failures, and thereby justifying discriminatory practices against specific social groups. Poor educational attainment is used to justify lack of success in the employment market: educational failures have only themselves to blame. Of course, if everyone achieved a high level of educational attainment, this would not improve overall employment rates: society would simply have to find a different rationale to allocate relatively scarce employment opportunities. This would simply be a more overt discrimination than the system currently used, where wealth and class are effectively used to monopolise most 'good' educational attainment.

Many current underlying ideologies and explanations for evident social disadvantages of different social groups thus place the 'blame' on the individual who fails, arguably overlapping with the meritocracy explanation. 'Pathological' explanations of failure include a claim that genetic disposition will determine intelligence (discounted by many leading geneticists, psychologists and child development experts); similarly, arguments based in the notion of 'transmitted deprivation' place the cause of failure of specific groups on their upbringing or socialisation. An extension of placing the blame on the individual, it is now the entire family, especially the 'deficient' parents, who are the cause of the child's failure to attain equal educational levels. This notion of deprivation may even be extended to whole social or cultural groups, as can be seen with stereotypes associated with Roma populations – especially concerning the passing down of 'dysfunctional' family patterns and behaviours from generation to generation. Likewise, home-based factors linked to economic factors (e.g. availability of resources such as books), linguistic factors (the use of a language different from the school), or cultural factors (lack of study habits) have been put forth as explanations for educational inequity. Inevitably, policies that aim to 'remediate' or 'correct' such 'deficiencies' end up tagging the social group that they target with labels like 'learning-disabled' (Casanova 1990: 148).

Schools are very often stigmatised as the cause for social and educational inequality. Mismatched resources, curriculum and teaching strategies, along with filtering and assessing based on criteria from mainstream student-performance are seen as principal causes of educational inequity. Low teacher expectations have been shown to correlate with student underachievement. Other arguments link home and school factors within structurally determined inequality – disadvantages of specific groups stem from lack of cultural and monetary capital, combined educational structures that maintain and propagate inequalities. The discursive construction of inequality and its subsequent creation of social hegemony have also been put forth by post-structuralists as an explanation for social and educational inequality. We have laid out and tried to interrogate these various explanations while maintaining the position that all explanations necessarily stem from specific interpretations of reality (belief systems) concerning the underlying reasons for different levels of educational performance. It is also acknowledged that these explanations often overlap (even conflicting ones), thereby resulting in ambiguous or even conflictive policies and practices.

Apart from these diverse explanations - and at times allocation of blame - for diversity of educational outcomes and varying underlying motivations for policies and practices based on different ways of understanding reality, this book has also looked at the way in which groups are identified as subjects of educational inequalities. The existence of group inequality is a focus of the European Commission, especially concerning economic attainment and integration. This inequality is often linked to educational inequity in the same policies. We suggest here that, given real conditions of equality in education, no specific group would perform better or worse than any other group, ignoring individual differences that would average out across all groups in conditions of equality anyway. Thus, when a social group is found to have lower educational performance or attainment it must be assumed that this is due to some type of negative discrimination – which at times may be deliberate, although more often it is unintentional and in conjunction with broader social inequality. A predominant reason for this is competition between groups – the exclusion of one group ensures more hegemonic control for the other group. This exclusion can then be easily rationalised by placing blame on the lower-achieving group, as we have described.

Inclusion or exclusion of groups in order to gain or maintain hegemony signifies identification of groups and membership to those groups. It is argued here that groups are socially constructed and categorisation into one group or another, especially in educational policies and practices, are heuristic and generally based on these general social constructions. At the same time, assumed 'traits' of groups are constantly changing, just as individual membership to groups are fluid and often overlap. However, due to the nature of administrative change, policies and practices do not change at the same rhythm as the social construction of groups and group identity. A further complexity lies in the agency of membership: identification with, and membership to a group may be through individual choice of inclusion (e.g. declaration of ethnicity as a self-identity) or it may be assigned (e.g. declaration of gender at birth). We have put forth a more pragmatic approach, based on perceptions of inequality and difference in relation to policies and practices, which are in turn based on educational attainment. As it was argued earlier in the book, once a group has been defined, the group's overall educational performance can be analysed to determine the need (or not) for providing support measures to address causes for underperformance. Pragmatic identification also allows for tracking for the monitoring of effectiveness of the targeted measures.

Within this framework of pragmatic group definition, analysing the ways in which different groups suffer social disadvantages indicates that educational inequalities may intersect across groups and that the specific requirements for educational equality vary greatly according to context, even in the same groups. Therefore, policies and practices should address specific needs and should depart from an analysis of educational outcomes, not equal access or opportunity. At the same time, it is recognised that the identification of socially and educationally disadvantaged groups has inevitable social implications – for instance negative association of 'at-risk' groups by parents, teachers, peers and even self-identification. There are also sub-groups within these larger categorical groups, wherein different causes for educational disadvantage have not been identified (because the group is subsumed in a larger group) or who do not suffer disadvantage in relation to educational outcome.

Despite these inherent difficulties and potential conflicts in defining disadvantaged groups, it is necessary, at some point, to ensure a starting point for analysing the different causes of unequal educational outcomes. To that point, five categories were deployed to describe groups that are educationally disadvantaged: socio-economic, minority-ethnic, disability, gender and sexuality, and linguistic minority. These groups allowed for a heuristic device to examine the ways in which educational inequality exists on a macro-level although we do not suggest that there are necessarily deliberate policies of discrimination in these areas. We examine the ways in which the effects of existing policies create, sustain and may even accentuate the degree of disadvantage although we are not trying to suggest that these are necessarily deliberate discriminatory actions – in fact, at times remediating policies may have an adverse effect on a disadvantaged group. We also do not argue that these are the only groups that may suffer educational disadvantage or that the groups are exclusive of one from the other.

In our analysis, socio-economic disadvantage emerged as a major characteristic of educational disadvantage, it is an intersecting and underlying trait in several of the groups discussed in this book. Still, poverty is a relative term (relative to period of time, overall conditions of the rest of society, and current prices for material goods, for instance). It is not the *sine qua non* of educational disadvantage, nor should it be seen as the only cause for educational disadvantage as this can lead to 'blame' when economic compensation is provided and members of this group still have lower educational performance.

Members of minority ethnic groups often suffer educational inequality; however, these particular groups are identified differently within different countries in the European Union. In some states, such groups are not officially identified, as this is held to be a type of racial profiling, in other countries the term may be applied to groups that have lived in the country for several generations and at times, the term may be blurred with long-standing indigenous populations, such as the Roma populations. Increasingly members of minority ethnic groups are intermarrying with members of the 'indigenous' population. Similarly, the term 'disability' has recently begun to encompass a wide range of sub-groups that may or may not include physical impairments, such as mental illnesses, permanent or temporary psychological disorders or, in some cases, learning obstacles. In some countries, those identified as having special education needs can encompass as a matter of course immigrant students or students whose family tongue is different from the school. Gender and sexuality as forms of educational disadvantage, define individuals, like members of other groups, according to closely tied and deeply ingrained social attitudes. Stereotypical attitudes within the classroom, in institutionalised policies, in implicit expectations and so on can lead to unequal educational outcomes. Nonetheless, such categories – especially in the wide area of gender equality- have been the focus of extensive policy-making in the European Union. Linguistic minorities can suffer from educational practices that discriminate against languages other than the mainstream. Such groups may include minority languages with established historical ties to a particular region(s) within a country or to groups whose language communities have been recently established, following migration.

We have also described the challenges that arise in determining whether a particular group is suffering from some form of educational inequality. A systematic comparative study that examines the processes of education is impractical to carry out across countries, just as qualitative case studies would require enormous human and economic resources and could not necessarily be extrapolated for general use. Our approach, through policy analysis and evaluation of outcomes, supported by numerous cases studies (in the original EPASI study) provides accounts of educational inequality, although not necessarily covering all the gaps between policy intentions and implementation. Indeed, the focus on educational outcomes rather than educational opportunities is not as straightforward as would be desired since how and how much data is collected in different countries varies widely, not to mention the diverse categories used in different countries means that data is not necessarily grouped or filed in similar fashion, rendering a full comparison of outcomes across countries extraordinarily difficult.

For these reasons, seven indicators of educational inequality were chosen – markers that can be examined to analyse outcomes across groups (and within groups as is the case of lower or higher literacy levels between different immigrant groups, see chapter three). These seven indicators are functional literacy levels, participation in post-compulsory education and/or training, participation in higher education, employment, school exclusion (temporary suspensions, full exclusion), social exclusion and bullying, and structural barriers (streaming, pressure for specific academic tracks, etc.). There are different responses to such evidence that educational inequality exists, for instance, denial that the problem exists or evasion from responsibility of cause or for solution.

Even when there is institutional acknowledgement of educational inequality, actions can have repercussions that do not necessarily remedy the situation of inequity. It has already been argued that the competiveness of market capitalism can provoke situations of social inequality through control of the educational curricula, policy and practice as well as access to desired forms of cultural capital. However, the agency of individuals within a complex, dynamic system (as is education within the social fabric of a given society) should not be underestimated and the hegemonic infrastructure should not be seen as a top-down imposition of 'the powerful majority' which never meets resistance. In fact, such hierarchies are made up of so many different structures - discourse, ideologies, power relations, individual and social values, perceptions, and an endless list of other factors - that an assumed unidirectional impact of just one factor does not stand up to rigorous scrutiny. Still, it stands to reason that dominant discourses that emerge from power-holders such as government, industry and the upper class are more likely to reflect the interests of the ruling class while minority groups are less likely to be represented in dominant discourse (Jenks, 2005).

Different intersecting discourses – such as public, institutional and *vox populi* - can have an impact on the ways in which inequality is defined, perceived and dealt with in specific contexts and may result in conflictive policies and practices. In European documents it is not uncommon to find 'diversity' defined and perceived as a cultural capital to be maintained and promoted while at the same time the notion of diversity is linked to the cause of educational and social inequality that must be dealt with.

Discursive intersectionality can also have an impact on how groups are defined and who is included. Membership into a specific group (often accomplished discursively) can result in labelling, reinforcement of negative self-identity, lower expectations or allocation of blame for assumed deficiencies of the group (again, features that are often socially constructed through different available discourses). Labelling of groups with general, discursive features (e.g. poor, immigrant) can also mask specific needs or abilities of groups subsumed in that group, just as 'meritocracy' discourse can facilitate and justify access for some groups to educational opportunities while effectively barring access (and placing the onus of 'effort and perseverance' on others).

Inclusion in certain groups can also lead to individual actions that have an effect on other populations. As we discussed in chapter four, the

identification of a population in need of intervention and support can lead
the majority population to take actions such as withdrawing from the
school, resulting in ghettoes. As students or their parents flee from these
schools into private schools where there are more material and human
resources, popular discourse of 'underachieving' minority school versus
academic 'excellence' becomes reinforced. Schools with perceived lower
academic quality may have a negative socialising effect on the students
and teachers themselves in several ways; lowered expectations in the
curriculum   with less challenging content, lower expectations by the
teachers and students, assumptions of 'pathological' or 'home-based'
deficiencies, provision of less resources, and lowered motivation of the
entire school population. This extends to the notion of ´naturalised'
discourse that 'problematises' specific groups, such as the classification by
teachers of minority-ethnic groups as 'difficult' to teach; discourse which
can eventually become 'naturalised' discourse for the same group and
debilitate any efforts to empower these groups. Lowered self-expectations
may also be reinforced in situations where teacher's assumptions of
'appropriate' social and academic behaviour does little to recognise and
reinforce specific students' competences that may not be considered
'mainstream' (e.g. a student's oral competence in French in Spanish-
speaking schools, see Dooly 2009).

But the concept of 'a school for all' is prey to inconsistencies between the
implementation of politically decided measures and outcomes which very
often appear to be no more than superficial cosmetic paper reforms.
Pointing out and discussing groups as 'having' various kinds of problems
without linking it to wider social policies and economic reforms creates a
question of credibility. We suggest that a shift from labelling individuals
in this way would be appropriate, and would want to see research
initiatives that have the clear purpose of examining and proposing
solutions to what we would define as societal rather than individual
problems.

It is extremely serious that 'the freedom of choice' principle and the
emergence of an increasing number of schools being driven by
competition and profit motives has lead to some students being regarded
of little value to the school. It is clear that political decisions to let the
market set the agenda for how to run schools has had negative
consequences for schools that are characterised by diversity by creating a
lack of symbolic capital in those schools. There is also a risk that this in
turn leads to a sense of resignation amongst those who work in diversity

schools. Both teachers and children may feel that they are considered as being passed over, when others have moved on to schools with considerable higher status and often better resources.

It is relevant to ask why there has been such little political interest in looking for evidence that the changes from when society was responsible for the school as a whole to a sometimes aggressive marketisation have had the desired effect. The ideological overtones may be too fragile to withstand close scrutiny: but this is another area that calls for regular evaluation and research.

Many international policy documents and declarations explicitly place the child in the foreground, emphasising the variety of experiences and needs of the individual student, thus these needs should become the focus for the group. These multifaceted experiences and needs often explicitly require professionals to adopt a *child perspective,* making sure their professional expertise is regularly updated on the needs of children and young people in special needs, those living in poverty, those finding school unchallenging (since they already 'know it all'), children and young people not belonging to the majority culture and speaking a different mother tongue than others in their class, and so on. The discussion on how to adopt an adequate child perspective should, we suggest, be part of the continuous and strategic planning in all schools.

While curricula in many countries are underlining the importance for schools to use diversity when planning and carrying out the educational work, we see very little evidence of the *child's perspective* coming to the foreground in the increasingly complex society in which they are supposed to become active participants. Being an active participant calls for a child or a young person actually being allowed to be vigorously involved. This is more than simply being fed the same uncontested content as generations before, with few links or relevance to life in the present. This requires teachers and students to cooperate in discussion and practice at all levels, and national evaluations might provide evidence for how this can be achieved.

If society really wants participative, empathetic and responsible citizens, exerting their rights and fulfilling their duties, then students must be allowed to be active, expressing their experiences, interests and needs in cooperation with others from childhood to adulthood. It is the creation of democratic education, and not simply education *about* or *for* democracy.

Democratic values, we argue, need to be habitually discussed, problematised and renegotiated.

Given the unprecedented poor conditions faced by Roma groups living in several European countries, and given the inexcusable manner in which school authorities, in for example the Czech Republic, treat Roma children and young people by indiscriminately placing them in special schools even if they do not fulfill any existing criteria for such placements, it is hard to even write a word such as *democracy*. This neglect of the Roma population applies to several European countries and needs to be moved to a higher European level, involving all countries.

We have also dealt with the concept of problem children and the consequences of the eager sorting of children and young people into 'normal' and 'deviant' groups. This can be analysed from a categorical or a relational perspective. We have shown that in a prosperous country like Sweden school authorities and schools to a shockingly high extent do not bother to find adequate information and fail to conduct adequate diagnoses of the specific levels of learning needs. Instead, children are allocated to special schools where they should not be. The proportion of pupils with foreign backgrounds is higher in special schools than in elementary school. This is critical to what opportunities a young person has when leaving school: doors to advanced education and finding work are closed. Continuous external investigations, of high quality, are needed, coupled with mechanisms for families to appeal against school placements. There will inevitably be costs to support those affected when they have to catch up or supplement their education.

The official and lame excuses for the bundling together and treating of individuals in groups labeled Roma, ethnic minority, with special needs etc., and the evasions of finding adequate solutions for each individual, have devastating consequences for vulnerable children and young people. We ask ourselves if it is really possible to talk about 'a school for all' or if the Shibboleth tradition of separating 'them' from 'us' is too strong to break even in societies calling themselves democracies.

Towards solutions

Throughout this book we have highlighted the challenges of attempting to define groups that suffer inequality and trying to delineate the causes for educational inequity. Endeavouring to put forth ways of addressing these inequities is equally complex. A 'menu' of suggestions and tips to choose from is not an option. Solutions are part of the highly complex, interrelated organisation that makes up the educational system, the policies and practices that govern and emerge from it as well as society in general.

We begin with some specific proposals about targeted interventions – which should always be planned and carried out with the concerned disadvantaged communities - and then move on to conclude with some more fundamental suggestions for reform, that we suggest are necessary to underpin strategies of success and to transform the climate of expectations.

1. Collect statistical and qualitative data on all aspects of underachievement

It is critical that qualitative and quantitative data are collected and analysed about educationally underperforming groups. Policy interventions cannot operate in situations where we do not know who is not achieving as well, about how they are underachieving, and about what the barriers appear to be. So much greater attention needs to be given, at national and European levels, to the statutory collection of statistics about disadvantaged groups: who are they, where are they found, what structural disadvantages do they suffer under, what particular educational support do they need?   There will inevitably be difficulties about the degree of precision that is possible, but there is a need for pragmatism. Data will help identify the extent of inequalities; help determine the distribution of resources; and will allow the evaluation of any interventions. At the same time, this should not be misconstrued as an argument for 'performance ranking' that can be used for supporting educational policies based on meritocracy.

2. Set clear targets for who will be worked with, and what should be achieved

Targets in some cases that we examined seemed to have been imprecise, leading to confusion and sometimes frustration amongst the educational professionals. Identifying the group, the nature of what the difficulties are, the areas to be addressed and the outcomes to be achieved, will help focus activity. Arguably, this can only be effective if all potentially targeted groups are involved from the beginning in the diagnosis and policy planning.

3. Measure real outcomes, not proxies

Policy should be based on measures of outcome, take-up and need, rather than on other measures that are taken to stand for these items. This will mean that attention is focussed on achieving real outputs, rather than on proxies for them.

4. Evaluate, learn from success, modify

Every programme should have planned, from its inception, mechanisms to evaluate the activity. Evaluation should be an iterative activity, and should involve internal team members and an external supportive critical focus. We saw many projects where analysis was missing, post hoc or cursory. Findings were not fed back into project management, or were ignored. Again, involvement of the target audience should be a backbone not only to the implementation but to the evaluation.

5. Institutionalise programmes so they support all practitioners

Programmes delivered by potentially isolated specialists encourage practitioners to think of these pupils as 'different', who can only be supported by specialist teachers in specialist structures. This isolates the group being targeted: we must make diversity mainstream.

6. Where intervention programmes are successful, consider adapting them to use in other appropriate contexts

If an initial programme has positive effects, there should be consideration given to how it might be modified and adapted to make it appropriate to use on a larger scale. John Rawls wrote that resources for education should not be allotted on the basis of economic returns, but 'according to their worth in enriching the personal and social life of citizens, including the less favoured' (Rawls, 1971, p 107).

7. Take a long term view of success and change

Educational processes take time. It takes many years to educate a child, and many more years to change the completely teaching workforce. Programmes – and expectations of their full results – should be planned with this in mind.

8. Work with a range of agencies, at a range of levels, in a range of areas

Multi-agency working (including community and voluntary groups, particularly from the communities concerned) is more likely to produce coordinated action that reaches more pupils at risk, and approaches them with a variety of support strategies.

However, these interventions are far more likely to succeed if we also address the prevailing climate of expectations that particular groups will fail in education. This brings us to the most useful concept of supply-side and demand-side failures in educational provision for equity: Nicaise's (2000) suggestion that inequalities in educational outcomes arise from two related forms of failures. Failures on the demand side arise where the socio-economic characteristics of social groups lead to individuals from these groups declining to take up educational opportunities. Failures on the supply side occur where educational policies and practices lead to disadvantageous treatment of members of a group in the educational process (including both institutional prejudice against these groups and the inability of institutions to respond actively to the specific and different needs of particular groups).

If the 'supply side' institutions cannot adequately support the group, then they create a situation in which members of the group lower their aspirations and expectations of success, and make fewer demands on the educational system. We have suggested that many teachers, schools, governments – and society itself – have low expectations of underperforming groups: and members of underperforming groups need to be supported in expecting that they will achieve educationally. These expectations and beliefs are extraordinarily powerful in maintaining inequity.

This is the underlying fundamental challenge: to change the expectations of an underperforming group into an expectation of success. There are three fora of expectation: members of the group itself – students, parents, community leaders; the educational professions – teachers, principals, policy-makers; and the public at large, the whole population. Each of these three needs to expect that young people in the group will achieve, as a matter of course, just as well as the norm. We have shown how feelings of inferiority pervade underperformance and poor expectations of any one of these three – students, teachers, the public – insidiously feed each other, creating a climate of failure.

There is a need to ensure that members of disadvantaged groups are empowered to expect and demand the specific educational resources and programmes needed in order to achieve equality of outcome. For parents, this may mean raising educational expectations of the possible attainment levels and then encouraging them to expect and demand the resources and support needed for continued education for their children. This also means getting specific groups involved in the planning and delivery of educational programmes in order to better articulate specific needs and social and cultural profiles with programmes and resources. Where communities are involved in identifying and defining issues, in planning and managing programmes, and in evaluation, the chances of success seem to be higher. It is not just their knowledge and experience that ensure culturally sympathetic approaches, but the deliberate empowerment of communities, giving them agency.

Parallel to this, there is a need to educate the majority population about the needs and rights of minorities in a diverse and unequal society. By deconstructing the 'naturalised' discourse of the ineducability of disadvantaged groups, generalised expectations of lower achievement will no longer hold, nor will rationalisations or justifications for lower educational attainment of these groups. National and European programmes that make prejudice, racism, xenophobia and intolerance unacceptable behaviour would involve legislation and monitoring and adjudication systems, but also public information programmes and conspicuous and conscious attempts to ensure a fair representation of 'underperforming' minorities in all aspects of public life.

And within this process, it is critical that there is an explicit focus on the education professions. Teachers should be explicitly trained in understanding diversity and in examining their own beliefs about different student profiles that will inevitably effect their expectations of their pupils. There is often very little institutionalised training of this sort for general education students, most specific training for dealing with the groups named here are considered to be part of specialised teaching staff that deal specifically with these groups. This, in turn, leads a marginalization not only of the students (who are perceived as part of educational problems outside of mainstream) but also of the teachers who specialise in these fields. Thus, training in understanding cultural and other diversities, awareness-raising of the effects of teachers having low expectations of success and specific for improving educational performance in all groups must be included in pre-service education, and support programmes for the teachers who are already in post, in order to ensure faster results and social change.

In particular, education programmes should actively recruit from disadvantaged groups. Ensuring that there are representatives of all social and cultural groups helps education systems - in which students are immersed in the social process of learning from a very young age until they are almost fully adults - fully reflect the spectrum of cultural and social traditions and systems that make up society. It will also ensure that the teaching profession as a whole can match the range of cultural and social varieties that our society contains and which are represented in the increasingly diverse classrooms. In this way, the educational system can aspire that each individual student feels that her or his cultural set is acknowledged and valued, thus empowering her or him as a learner. Having a widely representative group of teachers helps counter explicit and implicit prejudice – be it racist, gendered, class-based, disability-focussed - in schools and other educational institutions. Teachers who may have suffered from forms of prejudice will be more likely to recognise different, at times subtle, forms of xenophobia, chauvinism and racism in society. Representation from diverse groups can also serve as aspirational role models for other members of these groups, helping children see that that minorities have as much power and prestige as any other citizen, and that they too can aspire to achievement and excellence. Just as importantly, it will convey the same message to children from the majority population.

THE AUTHORS:
BIOGRAPHICAL NOTES

Melinda Dooly teaches in the Science Education Faculty of the Universitat Autònoma de Barcelona (Spain). She teaches English as a Foreign Language Methodology (TEFL) and research methods courses, particularly focusing on telecollaboration in education. She has published in the areas of teacher education and carried out research in the area of citizenship education and identity. Within this area, she has edited and co-edited two books; published numerous articles and chapters and participated in a variety of European-funded projects.

Dr. Dooly has been a guest lecturer at several European and North American universities, and has participated in many international research and educational projects. She served as Head of International Relations at her faculty from 2001-2005, as National Coordinator for CiCe (Children's Identity and Citizenship Education) from 2002-2010 and as Head of Graduate Studies for her department from 2008-2011.

She is the founding Editor of *Bellaterra Journal of Teaching and Learning Language and Literature* and is co-editor of the book series *Telecollaboration in Education* (Peter Lang). She is also criticism and reviews Editor of *Language and Intercultural Communication Journal* and Scientific Committee Member of *Hechos y Proyectos de Lengua*.

Nanny Hartsmar is associate Professor of Pedagogy in the Faculty of Education and Society at Malmö University (Sweden). From the mid 1970s to the early 90s she worked as a primary teacher in schools in the city of Malmö. After that she became a teacher educator at what is now Malmö University.

Since 1998 she has been a member of the European Commission Academic Network CiCe (Children's Identity and Citizenship in Europe). She was CiCe national coordinator for Sweden for many years. She is an executive member of CiCe and CiCea, Children's Identity and Citizenship European association and President-elect of CiCea.

In 2006 she contributed to set up the multidisciplinary research environment in Malmö University Childhood, Learning and Didactics (CLaD). The learning and education of younger children has been highlighted in recent years in national and international education policy. The research within CLaD has a clear societal perspective, focussing on the development of knowledge about preschool and primary education, but also to other areas of learning for those aged between one and twelve. CLaD is designed specifically to be based on studies of contemporary childhood, and terms of children's learning and problematising the content of early learning.

She was part of the fourteen countries study EPASI, Charting Educational Policies to Address Social Inequalities in Europe 2006-2008. She was also contributing to the MIPEX project (2011) as a member of an expert group and as a reviewer of the Swedish data. She is currently working in the interregional (Sweden-Denmark) project INDEX, Education Design to Improve Life, which is focussing on democratic education, innovation and social entrepreneurship.

Alistair Ross is Jean Monnet *ad personam* Professor of Citizenship Education in Europe and Emeritus Professor at London Metropolitan University (UK). He began his professional career as a primary teacher in inner London, before moving to become a teacher educator.

He established the European Commission Academic Network CiCe (Children's Identity and Citizenship in Europe) in 1998, which linked over a hundred universities in 27 European countries in analysing issues of children and young people's social understanding. He coordinated this to 2008, and still maintains an interest in its development. In 2000 he set up the Institute for Policy Studies in Education at London Metropolitan University, which focuses on the analysis of policies that address social justice and challenge educational inequalities. Over a hundred funded projects were undertaken by the Institute while he was Director (to 2009), commissioned by local educational bodies, foundations and charities, the UK government, the European Commission and research councils and agencies.

In 2009 he stepped down as Director, and now works part-time for the Institute. He has carried out an analysis of educational policies in Europe that are directed at migrants (MIPEX, 2011), and is currently engaged in a one-person study of young peoples' constructions of identities (local, national and European) in fourteen European countries. He is a member of the group of experts advising the European Commission on the 2012 initiative on combating educational inequity.

BIBLIOGRAPHY

Aftonbladet (2011) Mobbade elever blir dubbelt kränkta. *Aftonbladet* (accessed at http://www.aftonbladet.se/debatt/debattamnen/skola/article8577127.ab, 16 February 2011)

Alesina, A. and Perotti, R. (1996) Income Distribution, Political Instability, and Investment, *European Economic Review*, 40(6) 1203–1228

Alesina, A. and Rodrik, A. (1994) Distributive Politics and Economic Growth. *Quarterly Journal of Economics*, 109 (2), 465 -490

Anderson, B. (1991 rev ed). *Imagined communities: reflections on the origin and spread of nationalism.* London: Verso

Anderson, P. (1984) *In the Tracks of Historical Materialism.* Chicago IL: University of Chicago Press

Apple, M. W. (1990) *Ideology and the Curriculum* (2nd edition) London: Routledge

Apple, M. (2001) Comparing Neo-Liberal projects and inequality in education. *Comparative Education*, 37, 4, pp 409-423

Archer, L. and Hutchings, M. (2000) 'Bettering Yourself'? Discourses of risk, cost and benefit in ethnically diverse, young working-class non participants' constructions in higher education. *British Journal of Sociology of Education*, 21, 4

Archer, L. Ross, A. and Hutchings, M. (2003) *Higher Education and Social Class.* London: Routledge Falmer

Arendt, H. (2004/1977). *Between past and future: Eight exercises in political thought.* Translated by Persson, A. Göteborg: Daidalos

Aristotle, (1962) *The Politics* (trans. T.A. Sinclair). Harmondsworth: Penguin

Armandaiz A. (2001) The impact of racial prejudice on the socialization of Mexican American students in public schools. *Equity and Excellence in Education*, 33(3), 59-63

Aronson, J., Steele, Salinas, M., Lustina, (1998) The Effects of Stereotype Threat on the Standardized Test Performance of College Students, in E. Aronson, (ed), *Readings About the Social Animal*, 8th edition, New York: Freeman

Assarsson, I. (2007) *Talet om en skola för alla: pedagogers meningskonstruktion i ett politiskt uppdrag*. Malmö: Lärarutbildningen, Malmö högskola

Atkinson, J. M., and Heritage, J. (eds) (1984) *Structures of social action*. London: Longman

Ball, S. (2003) *Class Strategies and the Education Market: The middle classes and social advantage*. London: Routledge Falmer

Ball, S., Bowe, R. and Gewirtz, S. (1994) Market forces and parental choice, in Tomlinson, S. (ed) *Educational Reform and its Consequences*, London, IPPR/Rivers Oram Press. pp. 13–25

Banfield, G. (2010) Marxism, critical realism and class: implications for a socialist Pedagogy, In D. Kelsh, D. Hill, and S. Macrine (eds), *Class in education. Knowledge, pedagogy subjectivity* (pp. 128-152). Oxford and New York: Routledge

Bankston, C., and Caldas, S. (2000) White enrollment in nonpublic schools, public school racial composition, and student performance. *Sociological Quarterly, 4* (4), 539-550

Beach, D. (2008) The Changing Relations between Education Professionals, the State and Citizen Consumers in Europe: rethinking restructuring as capitalization. *European Educational Research Journal 7*:2, 105-107

Behtoui, A. (2006) 'Om det hade föräldrar födda på 'rätt plats'. Om ungdomar med utländsk bakgrund i det svenska utbildningssystemet och på den svenska arbetsmarknaden', Bilga 2, *Rapport Integration*, Norrköping, Integrationsverket

Bennett. R., Gottesman, R. Rock, D., and Cerullo, F. (1993) Influence of behaviour perceptions and gender on teachers' judgements of students academic skill. *Journal of Educational Psychology*, 85, 347-356

Berger, P. and Luckmann, T. (1966) *The Social Construction of Reality: A Treatise in the Sociology of Knowledge*, Garden City, NY: Anchor

Bernstein, B. (1971) Class *Codes and Control: Vol 1: Theoretical studies towards a Sociology of Language*. London: Routledge and Kegan Paul

—. (1974) A critique of the concept of 'compensatory education', in Wedderburn, D. (ed) *Poverty, inequality and class structure* (pp 109-122). Cambridge: Cambridge University Press

—. (1975) *Class, Codes and Control: Vol 3: Towards a Theory of Educational Transmission* (2nd ed\). London: Routledge and Kegan Paul

Berthoud, R. (1983) Transmitted Deprivation: The Kite that Failed', *Policy Studies*, 3, 3, pp 151-69

Biesta, G. (2006) *Bortom lärandet. Demokratisk utbildning för en mänsklig framtid.* Lund: Studentlitteratur

Boaz, D. (1998) *Libertarianism A Primer.* London: The Free Press

Börjesson, M. and Palmblad, E. (2003) *I problembarnens tid. Förnuftets moraliska ordning.* Stockholm: Carlsson Bokförlag

Bourdieu, P. (1971) Intellectual field and creative project', in Young, M.F.D. (ed) *Knowledge and Control: New directions for the sociology of education.* London: Collier Macmillan

—. (1973) Cultural reproduction and social reproduction, in Brown, R. (ed) *Knowledge, Education and Cultural Change.* London: Tavistock

—. (1974) The school as a conservative force: scholastic and cultural inequalities. In Eggleston, J (ed) *Contemporary research in the sociology of education.* London: Methuen

—. (1993) *The field of cultural production.* Cambridge: Polity

Bourdieu, P. and Passeron, J-C (1977) *Reproduction in Education, Society and Culture.* Guilford: Sage

Bourdieu, P. *et al.* (1999) *The Weight of the World.* Cambridge: Polity Press.

Bowles, S. (1973) Understanding Unequal Economic Opportunity. *The American Economic Review* 63, 2, pp. 346-356

Bowles, S. and Gintis, H (1981) Contradiction and Reproduction in Educational Theory. In Barton, L. (ed) *Schooling, Ideology, and Curriculum.* Sussex: Falmer Press

Bowles, S. and Gintis, H. (1976) *Schooling in Capitalist America: educational reform and the contradictions of economic life.* London: Routledge and Kegan Paul

Bowles, S. and Gintis, H. (1988) Can there be a liberal philosophy of education in a democratic society? In Coles, M. (ed) *Bowles and Gintis Revisited: Correspondence and contradiction in educational theory.* London: Falmer

Breen, R. (2001) A Rational Choice Model of Educational Inequality. Estudio/Working Paper 2001/166 [October 2001] (accessed at http://www.march.es/ceacs/ingles/publicaciones/working/archivos/200 2_166.pdf, 9 December 2010)

Breen, R. and Goldthorpe, J. (1997) Explaining Educational Differentials: Towards a Formal Rational Action Theory, *Rationality and Society* 9, 3: 275-305; reprinted in Grusky, D. (ed) 2001 *Social Stratification: Class, Race and Gender.* Boulder CO: Westview Press

Brillat-Savarin, J-A. (1825) *Physiologie de Goût* (published in English as *The Physiology of Taste* (1915), New York, NY: Houghton Mifflin

Bronfenbrenner, M. (1973) Equality and Equity, *Annals of the American Academy of Political and Social Science.* 409 1. 9-23

Brophy, I., and Good, T. (1974) *Teacher-student relationships: causes and consequences.* New York: Holt, Rinehart and Winston

Brophy, J. (ed) 1998) *Expectations in the Classroom.* Amsterdam: Elsevier

Brown, P. and Compton, R. (1994) *Economic Restructuring and Social Exclusion.* London: UCL Press

Bunar, N. (2009) *När marknaden kom till förorten – valfrihet, konkurrens och symboliskt kapital i mångkulturella områdens skolor.* Lund: Studentlitteratur

Burchardt, T. and Vizard, P. (2007) *Definition of equality and framework for measurement: Final Recommendations of the Equalities Review Steering Group on Measurement,* Centre for Analysis of Social Exclusion Papers; London: LSE (accessed at http://econpapers.repec.org/paper/cepsticas/_2F120.htm, 17 December 2010)

Burns, T., and Shadoian-Gersing, V. (2010) The importance of effective teacher education for diversity. In OECD (eds.), *Educating teachers for diversity. Meeting the challenge* (pp. 19-40). Paris: OECD Publishing

CACE (Central Advisory Council for Education, England) (1967) *Children and their Primary Schools* [The Plowden Report] London: HMSO

Card, D., and Rothstein, J. (2007) Racial segregation and the black-white test score gap. *Journal of Public Economics, 91*(11-12), 2158-2184

Casanova, U. (1990) Rasoman in the classroom: Multiple perspectives of teachers, parents and schools. In Barona, A. and Garcia, E. (eds) *Children at risk: Poverty, minority status and other issues in educational equity.* (135 – 149) Washington DC: National Association of Child Psychologists

Cederberg, M. (ed) (2011) *Elevcoach i skolan Kunskapsstöd för socialt arbete i skolan – en exemplifierande forskningsöverblick.* Malmö : Malmö Stad. 35-47

Cederberg, M., Hartsmar, N. and Lingärde, S. (2009) *Educational policies that address social inequality. Thematic report: Socioeconomic disadvantage.* London: Institute for Policy Studies in Education. (accessed at http://www.epasi.eu/ThematicReportSOC.pdf, 1 December 2010)

Cederberg, M. and Lingärde, S. (2008a) *Country Report: Denmark. Educational Policies that Address Social Inequality.* London: Institute for Policy Studies in Education. (accessed at http://www.epasi.eu/CountryReportDK.pdf, 1 December 2010)

Christensen, E. and Sloth, D.A. (2005) *Børn med anden etnisk baggrund ved skolestart.* Copenhagen: Socialforskningsinstituttet

Clark, C., Dyson, A. and Milward, A. (1998) *Theorising Special Education.* London and New York: Routledge

Cole, M., and Maisuria, A. (2010) Racism and islamophobia in post 7/7 Britain: Critical race theory, (xeno-)racialization, empire and education – a Marxist analysis. In Kelsh, D., Hill, D. and Macrine, S. (eds.), *Class in education. Knowledge, pedagogy subjectivity.* Oxford and New York: Routledge pp 108-127

Coleman, J. (1966) *Equality of Educational Opportunity.* Ann Arbor, MI: Inter-university Consortium for Political and Social Research

—. (1968) Equality of Educational Opportunity. *Equity and Excellence in Education*, 6, 5, September. pp 19-28

Colley, L. (1992) *Forging the Nation 1707-1837.* London: Yale University Press

Comber, B. and Simpson, A. (2001) *Negotiating Critical Literacies in Classrooms.* Mahwah, New York: L Erlbaum Associates

Compton-Lilly, C. (2003) *Reading families: The literate lives of urban children.* New York: Teachers College Press

Connell, R. (1994) Poverty and Education, Harvard Educational Review, 64, 2, Summer

Council of Europe (1995) *European Framework Convention for the Protection of National Minorities.* Strasbourg: Council of Europe (accessed at http://conventions.coe.int/Treaty/en/Treaties/html/157.htm,   1 December 2011)

—. (2001) *Common European Framework of Reference.* Cambridge: Cambridge University Press

—. (2003) *Guide for the Elaboration of Educative Linguistic Policies in Europe: from linguistic diversity to plurilingual education.* Strasbourg: Council of Europe Publishing

—. (2011) *Discrimination on grounds of sexual orientation and gender identity in Europe.* Strasbourg: Council of Europe Publishing

Cummins, J. (1998) Bilingual education in the United States: Power, pedagogy and possibility. *The Review of Education, Pedagogy and Cultural Studies*, 20 (3), 255-270

——. (2000) *Language, power and pedagogy; Bilingual children caught in the crossfire.* Toronto: Multilingual Matters

Cyprus: Minister of Education and Culture (nd) *Report of Internal Evaluation of Pilot Operation of Areas of Educational Priority 2003 – 2006* Nicosia: Cyprus [in Greek]

Dagens Nyheter (2011) *Barn placeras felaktigt i särskolan av kommunerna.* (accessed at http://www.dn.se/debatt/barn-placeras-felaktigt-i-sarskolan-av-kommunerna, 31 January 2011)

Dahl, K. M. (2005) *Etniske minoriteter i tal.* Copenhagen: Socialforskningsinstituttet

Dale, R., Esland, G. and MacDonald, M. (eds) (1976) *Schooling and Capitalism; A sociological reader.* London: Routledge and Kegan Paul/Open University Press

Davies, B. (1993) *Shards of glass: Children reading and writing beyond gendered identities.* Sidney: Allen and Unwin

Davis, B., and Sumara, D. (2006) *Complexity and education: Inquiries into learning, teaching and research.* New Jersey: Lawrence Erlbaum Associates

Dearing, E., Berry, D. and Zaslow, M. (2006) Poverty During Early Childhood. in McCartney, K. and Phillips, D. (eds.) *Blackwell Handbook of Early Childhood Development.* Oxford: Blackwell Publishing, pp. 399-423

Debraj, R. (1998) *Development Economics.* Princeton, NJ: Princeton University Press

Department for Education and Skills (2006) *Ethnicity and Education: The Evidence on Minority Ethnic Pupils aged 5–16 (Research Topic paper 2006).* London: Department for Education and Skills. (accessed at http://www.dcsf.gov.uk/research/data/uploadfiles/0208-2006DOM-EN.pdf, 12 January 2009

Dewey, J. (1916) *Democracy and Education.* New York: Macmillan

Diamond, P. and Giddens, A. (2005) Accumulation of wealth is unjust where it arises not from hard work and risk-taking enterprise, but from "brute luck" factors such as returns from property. *New Statesman* (London. 27 June 2005)

Dooly, M, Vallejo, C. with Unamuno, V. (2009) *Linguistic Minorities Thematic Report. Educational Policies that Address Social Inequality.* London: Institute for Policy Studies in Education. (accessed at http://www.epasi.eu/ThematicReportLIN.pdf, 1 December 2010)

Dooly, M. and Vallejo, C. (2008) *Educational Policies that Address Social Inequality. Country Report: Spain.* London: Institute for Policy Studies in Education. *(accessed at* www.epasi.eu, 1 August 2011)

Dooly, M. (2009) *Doing Diversity. Teachers' Construction of Their Classroom Reality.* Bern: Peter Lang

Dooly, M. and Vallejo, C. (2008) *Country Report: Spain. Educational Policies that Address Social Inequality* London: Institute for Policy Studies in Education. (accessed at http://www.epasi.eu/CountryReportES.pdf, 1 December 2010)

Dovemark, M. (2004) *Ansvar - flexibilitet - valfrihet : en etnografisk studie om en skola i förändring* [thesis]. Göteborg: Acta Universitatis Gothoburgensis, 2004

Durkheim, E. (1897) (1956) *Suicide: A study in sociology.* London: Routledge and Kegan Paul

—. (1938) *L'evolution pedagogique en France.* Paris: Acan [Trans P Collins, *The evolution of educational thought: lectures on the formation and development of secondary education in France.* London: Routledge (1977)]

Emanuelsson, I., Persson, B. and Rosenqvist, J. (2001) *Forskning inom det specialpedagogiska området – en kunskapsöversikt.* Stockholm: Skolverket

Enkvist, I. (2000) *Feltänkt en kritisk granskning av idébakgrunden till svensk utbildningspolitik.* Stockholm: SNS förlag

Étienne, R. *et al.* (2008) *Educational Policies that Address Social Inequalities. Country Report: France.* London: Institute for Policy Studies in Education. (accessed at www.epasi.eu, 1 August 2011)

Eurocities Network (2010) *Social Exclusion and Inequalities in European Cities: Challenges and Response.* Brussels: Euro Cities

European Agency for Development in Special Needs Education (2003) *Key principles for Special Needs Education.* (accessed at http://www.european-agency.org/publications/ereports/key-principles-in-special-needs-education/keyp-en.pdf, 12 October 2011)

European Commission (1993) *Growth, Competitiveness, Employment: The challenges and the way forward into the 21st Century* COM(93) 70 [in the *Bulletin of the European Communities, Supplement 6/93*]. Luxembourg: Office for Official Publications of the European Communities

—. (1994) *European Social Policy - A Way Forward for the Union. A White Paper.* COM (94) 333 final, Luxembourg: European Commission. Directorate-General for Employment, Industrial Relations

—. (2003) *Investing in research: an action plan for Europe (*SEC(2003) 489) (Communication from the Commission)

—. (2004) *Integrating Immigrant Children into schools in Europe.* Brussels: Eurydice D/2004/4008/14 (accessed at http://eacea.ec.europa.eu/ressources/eurydice/pdf/0_integral/045EN.pd f, 20 January 2009)

—. (2007) *Inclusion Strategy of the 'Youth in Action' programme (2007-2013)*, CJ/05/2007-2-E. Brussels: DG Education and Culture

—. (2007) *Towards a more knowledge-based policy and practice in education and training (*SEC(2007) 1098) (Commission Staff Working Document). Brussels: European Commission

—. (2008) *Migration and mobility: challenges and opportunities for EU education systems* (Green Paper COM(2008) 423 final) (3 July 2008 SEC(2008) 2173). Brussels: European Commission

—. (2010) *Investing in research: an action plan for Europe* [SEC(2003) 489] (COM/2003/0226 final). Brussels: European Commission

Council of Europe (1995) *European Framework Convention for the Protection of National Minorities.* Strasbourg: Council of Europe (accessed at

http://conventions.coe.int/Treaty/en/Treaties/html/157.htm, 1 December 2011)

European Union (2000) *Presidency Conclusions, Lisbon European Council* (23-24 March). Brussels: European Union

—. (2009) Council conclusions of 26 November 2009 on the education of children with a migrant background (2009/C 301/07). *Official Journal of the European Union* C 301/5 11 December 2009. Brussels: European Union

Eurydice (2009) *Gender Differences in Educational Outcomes: Study on the Measures Taken and the Current Situation in Europe.* Brussels: Education, Audiovisual and Culture Executive Agency

Evans, G. (2004) The Environment of Child Poverty. American Psychologist, 59, 2, pp 77 -92

—. (2006) *Educational Failure and Working Class White Children in Britain.* Basingstoke: Palgrave

Evans, M.D.R., Kelley, J., Sikora, J., Treiman, D. (2010) Family scholarly culture and educational success: Books and schooling in 27 nations. *Research in Social Stratification and Mobility*, 28, 2, 171 – 197

Fairclough, N. (1989) *Language and power.* London: Longman

—. (1995) *Critical discourse analysis: The critical study of language.* Harlow: Longman

Fairlie, R., and Resch, A. (2002) Is there 'white flight' into private schools? Evidence from the National Educational Longitudinal Survey. *Review of Economics and Statistics, 84* (1), 21-33

Farrell, J. (1999) Changing conceptions of equality of education: forty years of comparative evidence. in Arnove, R. and Torres, C., *Comparative education: the dialectic of the global and the local.* Maryland: Rowman and Littlefield. 149 – 178

Ferguson, R. (1998) Can schools narrow the black-white test score gap? In C. Jencks and M. Phillips (eds), *The black-white test score gap.* Washington, D.C.: The Brookings Institution

Foucault, M. (1986) *Vansinnets historia under den klassiska epoken.* Lund: Arkiv Förlag

Fowler, R. (1991) *Language in the news: Discourse and ideology in the press.* London: Routledge

Fowler, R., Hodge, B., Kress, G. and Trew, T. (1979) *Language and control.* London: Routledge

Francis, B (2007) Negotiating the Dichotomy of Boffin and Triad: British-Chinese Pupils' Constructions of 'Laddism'. *Sociological Review* 2005, 53, 3

Friedman, M. (1990) *Free to Choose: A Personal Statement.* New York: Harvest Books

Friedman, M. (2002) *Capitalism and Freedom.* Chicago IL: University of Chicago Press

Garnett, B. (2010) Diversity in education: The importance of disaggregating data. in OECD (Eds), *Educating teachers for diversity. Meeting the challenge* (pp. 93-116). Paris: OECD Publishing.

Gee, J. P. (1996) *Social linguistics and literacies: Ideology in discourses* (2nd ed.). London ; Bristol, PA: Taylor and Francis

—. (2005) *An introduction to discourse analysis: Theory and method* (2nd ed.) London ; New York: Routledge

Geurts, E. and Lambrechts, B. (2008) *Country Report: The Netherlands, Educational Policies that Address Social Inequality.* London: Institute for Policy Studies in Education. (accessed at http://www.epasi.eu/CountryReportNL.pdf, 1 December 2010)

Gewirtz, S., Ball, S. and Bowe, R. (1995) *Markets, choice, and equity in education.* Maidenhead: Open University Press/McGraw-Hill

Giddens, A. (1984) *The Constitution of Society. Outline of the Theory of Structuration.* Cambridge: Polity Press

—. (1991) Structuration Theory. Past, Present and Future. In: Bryant, C. and Jary, D. (eds). *Giddens' Theory of Structuration. A Critical Appreciation.* London: Routledge

Giddens, A. and Diamond, P. (2005) *The New Egalitarianism.* London: Policy 2005

Gillborn, D. and Youdell, D. (2000) *Rationing education: Policy, practice, reform and equity.* Buckingham: Open University Press

Gillborn, D. (1990) *Race, ethnicity and education: Teaching and learning in multi-cultural schools.* London: Routledge Falmer

Gini, C. (1912) *Variabilità e mutabilità* [Variability and Mutability]. Bologna: Cuppini (reprinted 1955 in *Memorie di metodologica statistica* (ed. Salvemini, P) Rome: Libreria Eredi Virgilio Ves)

Goffman, E. (1963) *Stigma.* Harmondsworth: Penguin

Goldthorpe, J. (2010) Analysing Social Inequality: A Critique of Two Recent Contributions from Economics and Epidemiology *European Sociological Review*, 26(6): 731-744

Good, T. (1987) Two decades of research on teacher expectations: Findings and future directions. *Journal of Teacher Education*, 38, 4, pp 32-47

Goodson, I. and Sikes, P. (2001) *Life History in Educational Settings: Learning From Lives,* Buckingham, Open University Press

Gordon, D., Levitas, R., Pantazis, C., Patsios,D., Payne, S., Townsend, P., Adelman, L., Ashworth, K., Middleton, S., Bradshaw, J.and William, J. (1999) *Poverty and social exclusion in Britain.* York: Joseph Rowntree Foundation

Gramsci, A. (1971) *Selections from the prison notebooks of Antonio Gramsci* (trs Quintin Hoare and Geoffrey Nowell-Smith). London: Lawrence and Wishart

Griffin, C. (1993) *Representations of Youth: the study of youth and adolescence in Britain and America.* Cambridge: Polity Press

Grisay, A. (1984) Les mirages de l'evaluation scolaire, in *Review de la Direction Generale de l'Organisation des Etudes*, XIX, 8

Grosvenor, I. (1989) Teacher racism and the construction of black underachievement. in R. Lowe (ed) *The Changing Secondary School,* Lewes: Falmer

Haar, J. with Nielsen, T., Hansen, M. and Jakobsen, S. (2005) Explaining student performance: Evidence from the international PISA, TIMSS and PIRLS surveys. Copenhagen: Danish Technological Institute (accessed at http://www.oecd.org/dataoecd/5/45/35920726.pdf, 30 January 2009)

Haladyna, T. M. (2002) *Essentials of standardized achievement testing. Validity and accountability.* Boston: Allyn and Bacon

Halldén, Gunilla (2003) Barnperspektiv som ideologiskt eller metodologiskt begrepp. *Pedagogisk Forskning i Sverige*, 2003, 8/1–2:12–23

Hamre, B., and Pianta, R. (2005) Can Instructional and Emotional Support in the First-Grade Classroom Make a Difference for Children at Risk of School Failure? *Child Development*, 76(5), 949–967

Hardman, M. (2010) *Is complexity theory useful in describing classroom learning?* Paper presented at The European Conference on Educational Research. Helsinki, 26 August 2010

Hargreaves, A. (2003) *Teaching in the Knowledge Society: education in the age of insecurity.* Maidenhead, PA: Open University

Hartman, L. (2011) *Konkurrensens konsekvenser. Vad händer med svensk välfärd?* (258-276). Stockholm: SNS Förlag

Hartsmar, N. and Jönsson, K. (2010) Lärandets vem, varför, vad och hur i förskolans och grundskolans tidiga år. in S. Persson and B. Riddersporre (eds) *Perspektiv på barndom och barns lärande. En kunskapsöversikt om lärande i förskolan och grundskolans tidigare år.* Stockholm: Skolverket. pp 121-173

Hartsmar, N. (2001) *Historiemedvetande: elevers tidsförståelse i en skolkontext.* Malmö : Institutionen för pedagogik, Lärarhögskolan. Diss

—. (2008) *Educational Policies that Address Social Inequality. Country Report: Sweden.* London: Institute for Policy Studies in Education. (accessed at www.epasi.eu, 1 August 2011)

Hayek, F. (1976) *The Constitution of Liberty.* London: Routledge

Heckmann, F. (2008) *Education and Migration: Strategies for integrating migrant children in European schools and societies.* Lyon: Network of experts in Social Sciences of Education and training (NESSE) (accessed at http://www.interculturaldialogue2008.eu/fileadmin/downloads/resources/education-and-migration_bamberg.pdf, 30 January 2009)

Herrnstein and Murray (1994) *The Bell Curve.* Glencoe IL: Free Press

Hills, J., Le Grand, J. and Piachaud, D. (eds) (2002) *Understanding Social Exclusion*, Oxford, Oxford University Press, 2002

Ho, M-W (2001) *The Human Genome Map: The Death of Genetic Determinism and Beyond Synthesis.* Regeneration 25 (Summer 2001)

Hobsbawm, E. and Ranger, T. (eds) (1984) *The Invention of Tradition.* Cambridge: Cambridge University Press

Hoff, K. and Pandey, P. (2004) *Belief Systems and Durable Inequalities: An Experimental Investigation of Indian Caste.* Policy Research Working Paper. Washington DC: World Bank (accessed at http://sticerd.lse.ac.uk/dps/bpde2004/hoff.pdf, 28 August 2011)

Holloway, C. (2010) Relationality: the intersubjective foundations of identity. in Wetherell, M. and Mohanty, C. (eds) *Sage Handbook of Identities*. London: Sage. pp. 216-232

Holmberg, O. (2011) Vad gör socialdemokraterna medan högern kidnappar skolan? In *Skola och Samhälle, SOS*. (accessed at http://www.skolaochsamhalle.se/skolpolitik/olle-holmberg-vad-gor-socialdemokraterna-medan-hogern-kidnappar-skolan,   10   October 2011)

Holsinger, D. and Jacob, W. (2009) *Inequality in Education: Comparative and International Perspectives*. New York: Springer

Hoyles, M. (1977) Cultural deprivation and compensatory education, in Hoyles (ed) *The Politics of Literacy* p 172-181. London: Readers and Writers Publishing Cooperative

Huddleston, T., Niessen, J., Chaoimh, E. and White, E. (2011) *Migration Integration Policy Index III*. Brussels: British Council and Migration Policy Group

Interim Committee for the Australian Schools Commission (1973) *Schools in Australia*. Canberra: Australian Government Publishing Service

Jeffrey, J. R. (1978) *Education for the children of the poor: a study of the origins and implementation of the Elementary and Secondary education Act of 1965*. Columbus Ohio: Ohio State University Press

Jencks, J. (2001) Does inequality matter? *Daedalus*. 131, 49 – 65

Jenks, C. (2005) *Childhood*, 2nd ed. Oxford and New York: Routledge

Jonsson, G. (1969) *Det sociala arvet*. Stockholm: Tiden-Barnängen

Joseph, K. (1972) speech to the Pre-School Playgroups Association in June 1972, cited in Jordan, B. (1974) *Poor Parents: Social Policy and the 'Cycle of Deprivation*. London: Routledge and Kegan Paul

Kamali, M. (2006) Om social sammanhållning och dess hinder. in Masoud Kamali: *Den segregerande integrationen*. [SOU 2006:73] Stockholm: Statens Offentliga Utredningar

Kärfve, E. (2000) *Hjärnspöken: DAMP och hotet mot folkhälsan*. Mölndal: Brutus Östlings Bokförlag Symposiom

Kluegel. J. (1990) Trends in White's explanations of the Black-White gap in socio-economic status, 1977-1989, *American Sociological Review*, 33, pp 512 - 525

Kohn, A. (2005) Unconditional teaching. *Educational Leadership*, 63 (1) 20-24

Kumar, R. (2010) Persistent inequities, obfuscating explanations. Reinforcing the lost centrality of class in Indian education debates. In Kelsh, D., Hill, D. and Macrine, S. (eds), *Class in education*.

Knowledge, pedagogy subjectivity Oxford and New York: Routledge. pp. 66-86

Laclau, E. (1996) *Emancipation(s)*. London: Verso

—. (2005) *On populist reason*. New York: Verso

Lambrechts, B. with Geurts, E. and Verkest, H. (2008) *Country Report: Belgium (Flanders), Educational Policies that Address Social Inequality* London: Institute for Policy Studies in Education. (accessed at http://www.epasi.eu/CountryReportBE.pdf, 1 December 2010)

Lareau, A., and Horvat, E. (1999) Moments of social inclusion and exclusion: Race, class, and cultural capital in family-school relationships. *Sociology of Education*, 72, 37–53

Larsson, H.A. (2011) *Mot bättre vetande – en svensk skolhistoria*. Stockholm: SNS förlag

Lawton D and Gordon, P (1996) *Dictionary of Education* (2nd edn) London: Hodder and Stoughton

Leathwood, C., Ross, A., Moreau, M-P., Rollock, N. and Williams, C. (2008) *Country Report: The United Kingdom, Educational Policies that Address Social Inequality* London: Institute for Policy Studies in Education. (accessed at http://www.epasi.eu/CountryReportUK.pdf, 1 December 2010)

Leithwood, K. and Fullan, M. (2003) What should be the boundaries of the schools we need? *Education Canada*. 43(1), 12-15

Levitas, R. (1966) The concept of social exclusion and the new Durkheimian Hegemony. *Critical Social Policy*, 16. 1, pp 5 - 20

Lewis, O. (1963) The culture of poverty. *Society* 1 1 p 17 -19.

—. (1959) *Five Families: Mexican Case Studies in the Culture of Poverty*. New York: Basic Books

Liégeois, J.-P (2007) *Roms en Europe*. Paris: le Documentation française

Lindblom, J., and Ziemke, T. (2008) Interacting socially through embodied action. in F. Morganti, F, Carassa, A. and Riva, G. (eds) *Enacting intersubjectivity. A cognitive and social perspective on the study of interactions*. Amsterdam: IOS Press. pp. 49-63

Local Government Association (2008) Narrowing the Gap, Final Guidance Year 1 . London: C4EO, LGA

Lykke, N. (2005) Nya perspektiv på intersektionalitet: problem och möjligheter. *Kvinnovetenskaplig tidskrift*, 2-3 (7-17)

MacDonald, M. (1977) *Curriculum and Cultural Reproduction* [E202 Block 3] Bletchley: Open University Press

Macrine, S., Hill, D. and Kelsh, D. (2010) Introduction. in Kelsh, D., Hill, D. and Macrine, S. (eds), *Class in education. Knowledge, pedagogy subjectivity*. Oxford and New York: Routledge. pp. 1-5

Mannheim, K. (1936) *Ideology and Utopia*. London: Routledge and Kegan Paul

Mannitz, S. (2004a) Limitations, Convergences and Crossovers, in Schiffauer, W., Baumnann, G., Kastoryano, R. and Vertovec, S. (eds) *Civil Enculturation: Nation-state, schools and ethnic difference in four European countries*. New York: Berghahn, pp 307 - 333

Mannitz, S. (2004b) Pupils' Negotiations of Cultural Difference: Identity Management and Discursive Assimilation, in Schiffauer, W., Baumann, G., Katoryano, R. and Vertovec, S. (eds) *Civil Enculturation: Nation-State, School and Ethnic Difference in The Netherlands, Britain, Germany and France*. Oxford: Berghahn pp 242 - 303

Manuel-Navarrete, D. (2003) *Approaches and implications of using complexity theory for dealing with social systems*. Unpublished doctoral thesis. Department of Geography. University of Waterloo

Marion, R. (1999) *The edge of organization. Chaos, complexity theories and formal social systems*. London: Sage Publications.

McKenna, B. (2004) *Critical Discourse Studies: Where to from here?* Critical Discourse Studies, 1(1), 9-40

McLaren, P. (2010) Afterword. The contradictions of class and the praxis. in Kelsh, D., Hill, D. and Macrine, S. (eds), *Class in education. Knowledge, pedagogy subjectivity*. Oxford and New York: Routledge

McLeod, J. and Fettes, D. (2007) Trajectories of failure: The educational careers of children with mental health problems. *American Journal of Sociology*, 113(3), 653–701

Merton, R. (1948) The self-fulfilling prophecy. *Antioch Review*, 8, 193-210

Meyer, J. (1977) The effects of education as an institution. *American Journal of Sociology*, 83, 55 - 77

Mickelson, R. A. (2001) Subverting Swann: First- and second-generation segregation in the Charlotte-Mecklenburg schools. *American Educational Research Journal, 38* (2), 215-252

Micklewright, J. (2003) Education, inequality and transition. *Economics of Transition.* 7, 2, pp 343 - 376

Mitchell, K. (2006) Neoliberal governmentality in the European Union: Education, training and technologies of citizenship. *Environment and Planning D: Society and Space.* London: Kluwer Academic Publishers

Moldenhawer, B. (2001) *En bedre fremtid: Skolens betydning for etniske minoriteter*. Copenhagen: Hans Reitzels Forlag

Moreau, Marie-Pierre (2008) 'Plus ça change, plus c'est la même chose?': A cross-national comparison of gender inequalities in the teaching profession. in Olesky, E., Petö, A. and Waaldijk (eds), *Gender and Citizenship in a Multicultural Context*. Frankfurt: Peter Lang

Mortimore, P., Sammons, P., Stoll, L., Lewis, D. and Ecob, R. (1988) *School matters: The junior years*. Somerset: Open Book

Mulderigg, J. (2007) *Equality and Human Rights: Key concepts and issues*. Edinburgh: University of Edinburgh - Centre for Research in Education Inclusion and Diversity. (accessed at http://eprints.lancs.ac.uk/1274/1/Equality_and_Human_Rights_07.pdf, 12 July 2011)

Muller, A. and Beardsmore, H.B. (2004) Multilingual practice in plurilingual classes – European school practice. *Bilingual Education and Bilingualism, 7* (1), 24-42

Murray (1984) *Loosing Ground*. New York: Basic Books

National Center for Education Statistics. (2005) *Parent and family involvement in education: 2002–03*. Washington, DC: National Center for Education Statistics

Ng, S. and Bradac, J. (1993) *Power in language*. Newbury Park: Sage

Nicaise, I. (ed) (2000) *The Right to learn: educational strategies for socially excluded youth in Europe*. Bristol: Policy Press

Nirje, B. (1970) The normalization principle: Implications and comments. *British Journal of Mental Subnormality, 16*, 62-70

—. (1980) The normalization principle. In Flynn, R. and Nitsch, K. (eds). *Normalization, social integration and community services*. Baltimore: University Park Press

—. (1999) How I came to formulate the normalization principle. in Flynn, R. and Lemay, R. (eds) *A Quarter-Century of Normalization and Social Role Valorization; Evolution and Impact*. Ottawa: University of Ottawa Press

Nozick, R. (1974) *Anarchy, state, and utopia*. New York: Basic Books

ODPM Office of the Deputy Prime Minister (2004) *Breaking the Cycle: Taking Stock of Progress and Priorities for the Future: A Report by the Social Exclusion Unit*, London, ODPM, 2004, pp. 10, 28, 73, 93, 138.

OECD (2006) *Starting Strong II, Early Childhood Education and Care*. (accessed at http://www.oecd.org/document/63/0,3746,en_2649_39263231_374167 03_1_1_1_1,00.html, 18 November 2011)

Ofsted (2004) *Achievement of Bangladeshi heritage pupils* (HMI 513). London: Ofsted

Ogbu, J. (1992) Adaptation to minority status and impact on school success. *Theory into practice*, 31(4): 287-295

Olmeida Reinoso, A. (2008) Middle-Class Families and School Choice: freedom versus equity in the context of a 'local educational market'. *European Educational Research Journal, 7/2:* 176-194

Peters, W. (1971) *A Class Divided*. Garden City NY: Doubleday

—. (1987) *A Class Divided: Then and Now*. New Haven CT: Yale University Press

Pinnock, K. (2001) *Denied a Future - the Right to Education of Roma, Gypsy and Traveller Children*. London: Save the Children

Popham, W. J. (2002) Right task, wrong tool. *American School Board Journal*, 189 (2), 19-22

Power, S. (2007) *EU Research in Social Sciences and Humanities* [European policy review on education]. Brussels: European Commission, Directorate-General for Research

Quinton, A. (1995) Conservativism, in Goodin, R. and Pettit, P (eds) *A Companion to Contemporary Political Philosophy*. Oxford: Blackwell

Rawls, J. (1971) *A Theory of Justice*. Oxford: Oxford University Press

Reardon, S., Yun, J., and Eitle, T. (2000) The changing structure of school segregation: Measurement and evidence of multiracial metropolitan-area school segregation, 1989-1995. *Demography, 37* (3), 351-364

Reay, D. (2004) 'It's all becoming a habitus': beyond the habitual use of habitus is educational research. *British Journal of Sociology of Education*. 25, 4, pp 431 - 444

—. (2006) The Zombie stalking English Schools: Social Class and Educational Inequality. *British Journal of Educational Studies*. 54, 3, pp 288 –307

Reay, D., David, M. and Ball, S. (2005) *Degrees of choice: social class, race, gender and higher education*. Stoke on Trent: Trentham Books

Rees, T. (1998) *Mainstreaming Equality in the European Union: Education, Training and Labour Market Policies*. London: Routledge

Renzulli, L. A., and Evans, L. (2005) School choice, charter schools, and white flight. *Social Problems* 52(3): 398–418

Richardson, P. and Boyd, R. (2005) *Not by genes alone: how culture transformed human evolution*. Chicago: University of Chicago Press

Rist, R. (2000) (reprinted; originally 1970) Student Social Class and Teacher Expectations: The Self-Fulfilling Prophecy in Ghetto Education. *Harvard Educational Review* 70 3 pp 257 - 302

Robbins, D. (1991) *The Work of Pierre Bourdieu: The practice of theory*. London: Macmillan

Rollock, N. (2007) Legitimising black academic failure: deconstructing staff discourses of academic success, appearance and behaviour. *International Studies in Sociology of Education*, 17 (3), 275-287

Rose, N. (1994) Medicine, History and the Present. in C. Jones and R. Porter (eds) *Reassessing Foucault: Power, Medicine and the Body.* London: Routledge

Rosenthal, R., and Jacobson, L. (1968) *Pygmalion in the Classroom.* New York: Holt, Rinehart and Winston

Ross, A. (2002) A Representative Profession: Ethnic Minority Teachers in M. Johnson and J. Hallgarten (eds) *From Victims of Change to Agents of Change: The Future of the Teaching Profession* , London: IPPR

—. (2008) *A European Education: Citizenship, identities and young people.* Stoke on Trent: Trentham

—. (2009) *Educational Policies that Address Social Inequality: Overall Report.* London: Institute for Policy Studies in Education. (accessed at www.epasi.eu, 1 August 2011)

—. (2011) Developing the Education strand in MIPEX, in Cunningham, P. and Fretwell, N. (eds) *Europe's Future: Citizenship in a Changing World.* London: CiCe

Rousseau, J-J. (1762, 1968) *The Social Contract*, trans. Maurice Cranston. London: Penguin

Runfors, Ann (2006) Fostran till frihet? Värdeladdade visioner, positionerade praktiker och diskriminerande ordningar. in Sawyer, L., and Kamali, M. (eds) *Utbildningens dilemma. Demokratiska ideal och andrafierande praxis. Rapport av Utredningen om makt, integration och strukturell diskriminering.* [SOU 2006:40]. Stockholm: Statens Offentliga Utredningar. pp. 135-165

Rutter, M, (2006) 'Keith Joseph's Claim on Transmitted Deprivation and What Followed from It', paper given at the 'Cycles of Disadvantage' conference, St Catherine's College, Oxford, 21 July 2006

Rutter, M. and Madge, N. (1976) *Cycles of Disadvantage: A Review of Research.* London: Heinemann

Rutter, M., Maughan, B., Mortimore, P. and Ouston, J. (1979) *Fifteen Thousand Hours: Secondary Schools and their Effects on Children.* London: Open Books

Ryan, W. (1976) *Blaming the Victim* (2nd ed). New York: Vintage Books

Sanandaji, N., Malm, A. and Sanandaji, T. (2010) *A critical analysis of how 'The Spirit Level' compares countries.* Originally published in Swedish by Skattebetalarnas Förening, the Swedish Taxpayers' Association; republished in English by the UK Taxpayers Alliance, London

Sawyer, L. and Kamali, M. (eds) (2006) *Utbildningens dilemma. Rapport av Utredningen om makt, integration och strukturell diskriminering.*

Demokratiska ideal och andrafierande praxis [SOU 2006:40]. Stockholm: Statens Offentliga Utredningar

Schiratzki, Johanna (2003) Barnkonventionen och barnets bästa – globalisering med reservation. I B. Sandin and G. Halldén (eds) *Barnets bästa – en antologi om barndomens innebörder och välfärdens organisering*. Stockholm/Stehag: Brutus Östlings bokförlag Symposion. pp 25–52

Sen, A (1999) *Development as Freedom*. New York: Anchor Books

—. (1980) 'Equality of What?', in: *The Tanner Lecture on Human Values*, vol. I, Cambridge: Cambridge University Press, pp. 197-220, reprinted in A. Sen, *Choice, Welfare, and Measurement*, Oxford: Blackwell 1982

—. (1985) *Commodities and Capabilities*. Oxford: Oxford University Press

—. (1992) Inequality Re-examined. Cambridge, MA: Harvard University Press

—. (2009) *The Idea of Justice*. Cambridge MA: Harvard University Press

Sikes, P. (2008) At the Eye of the Storm: An Academic(s) Experience of Moral Panic. *Qualitative Inquiry* 14, 2, pp. 235 -253

Silver, H. and Silver, P (1991) *An educational war of poverty: American and British policy-making 1960-1980*. Cambridge: Cambridge University Press

Sivertsen, M.B. (2007) *Hvordan virker indsatsen mod negative social arv?* København: Socialforskningsinstituttet

Skidmore, D. (1996) Towards an integrated theoretical framework for research into special education needs. *European Journal of Special Needs Education*, 14(1), 12-20

Skolinspektionen (2011a) *Särskolan: Granskning av handläggning och utredning inför beslut om mottagande* [2010:259]. Stockholm: Skolinspektionen

Skolinspektionen (2011b) *Olika elever - samma undervisning: Skolinspektionens erfarenheter och resultat från tillsyn och kvalitetsgranskning 2010* [40-2011:439]. Stockholm: Skolinspektionen

Socialstyrelsen (1993) *Lag om stöd och service till vissa funktionshindrade, LSS* [SFS-nr: 1993:38]. Stockholm: Socialstyrelesen, (accessed at http://www.socialstyrelsen.se/publikationer2007/2007-114-49/Documents/2007-114-49_200711429.pdf, 10 October 2011)

Sohoni, D., and Saporito, S. (2009) Mapping school segregation: Using GIS to explore racial segregation between schools and their corresponding attendance areas. *American Journal of Education, 115*(4), 569-600

Sonuga-Barke, E. J. (2010) Editorial: Editorial 'It's the *environment* stupid!' Onepigenetics, programming and plasticity in child mental health. *Journal of Child Psychology and Psychiatry,* 51: 2 pp 113

SOU (Statens Offentliga Utredningar) (2010) *'Se de tidiga tecknen': forskare reflekterar över sju berättelser från förskola och skola* [SOU 2010:64]. Stockholm: Statens Offentliga Utredningar

Spicker, P. (2006) *Liberty, Equality, Fraternity.* New York: Policy Press

Spinthourakis, J., Karatzia-Stavlioti, E., Lempesi, G-E. and Papadimitriou, I. (2008) *Country Report: Greece, Educational Policies that Address Social Inequality* (EACEA Action 6.6.2) London: Institute for Policy Studies in Education. (accessed at http://www.epasi.eu/CountryReportGR.pdf, 1 December 2010)

Stanat, P. and Christensen, G. (2006) *Where immigrant students succeed : A comparative review of performance and engagement in PISA 2003.* Paris: OECD (accessed at http://www.oecd.org/dataoecd/2/38/36664934.pdf, 30 January 2009)

Steele, C. and Aronson, J. (1995) Stereotype threat and the intellectual test performance of African Americans. *Journal of Personality and Social Psychology* 69 5 pp 797–811

Stipek, D., and Miles, S. (2008) Effects of aggression on achievement: Does conflict with the teacher make it worse? *Child Development,* 79 (6), 1721–1735

Strand, S. (in press) The White British-Black Caribbean achievement gap: Tests, tiers and teacher expectations, *British Educational Research Journal,* in press. (accessed T http://www2.warwick.ac.uk/fac/soc/cedar/staff/stevestrand/strand_inpr ess_tiering_prepub.pdf, 10 September 2011)

Strand, S., de Coulon, A., Meschi, E., Vorhaus, J., Frumkin, L., Ivins, C., Sood, A., Gervais, M-C., and Rehman H. (2010) *Drivers and Challenges in Raising the Achievement of Pupils from Bangladeshi, Somali and Turkish Backgrounds, London: Department of Families, Schools and Children* (Research Report DCSF-RR22)

Sunier, T. (2004) Argumentative Strategies, in Schiffauer, W., Baumnann, G., Kastoryano, R. and Vertovec, S. (eds) *Civil Enculturation: Nation-state, schools and ethnic difference in four European countries.* New York: Berghahn, pp 210 -241

Thrupp, M. (1995) The school mix effect: The history of an enduring problem in education research, policy and practice. *British Journal of Sociology of Education, 16*(2), 183-203

Tikly, L., Haynes, J, Caballero, C. and Hill, J. (2006) *Evaluating of Aiming High: African Caribbean Achievement Project*. DfES Research Report 801/2006. London: DfES

Townsend, P. (1979) *Poverty in the United Kingdom: a survey of household resources and standards of living*. Harmondsworth: Penguin Books

Tozzi, Pascal and Étienne, R. (2008) *Country Report: Luxembourg. Educational Policies that Address Social Inequality*. London: Institute for Policy Studies in Education.(accessed at http://www.epasi.eu/CountryReportLX.pdf, 1 December 2010)

Trondman, M. (2009) Mångkontextuella och gränsöverskridande lärprocesser: om barn som självreglerande och egenansvariga subjekt. *Educare Vetenskapliga Skrifter*. 2-3 241-298

UK (1998) School Standards and Framework Act. London: HMSO

UK (Home Office) (1999) The Stephen Lawrence Inquiry: Report of an inquiry by Sir William Macpherson. Cm 4262-I. London: The Stationary Office

Undervisningsministeriet (2005) *Tal der taler 2005*. accessed at http//pub.uvm.dk/2005/taldertaler, 19 November 2007

UNESCO (1994) *The Salamanca Statement and Framework for Action on Special Needs Education*. (accessed at http://www.unesco.org/education/pdf/SALAMA_E.PDF, 18 November 2011)

Vinnerljung B (1998) Socialt arv [Social heritage] in Denvall V and Jacobson T (eds) *Vardagsbegrepp i socialt arbete* [Common-sense-concepts in social work]. Stockholm: Norstedts Juridik.

Vlachos, J. Friskolor i förändring. In Hartman, L. (2011) *Konkurrensens konsekvenser. Vad händer med svensk välfärd?*. Stockholm: SNS Förlag. Pp 66-110

Vrabcova, Daniela, Vacek, P. and Lašek, J. (2008) *Country Report: The Czech Republic, Educational Policies that Address Social Inequality*. London: Institute for Policy Studies in Education.(accessed at http://www.epasi.eu/CountryReportCZ.pdf, 1 December 2010)

Wacquant, L. (1996) Foreword to Bourdieu, P. *The State Nobility*. Stanford: Stanford University Press. pp. ix–xxii

Wade, R. (2005) Does Inequality Matter? *Challenge* 48, 5 pp 12 - 38

Walby, S. (2007) *Complexity theory, systems theory, and multiple intersecting social inequalities*. Philosophy of the Social Sciences, 37 (4): 449-470

Walkerdine, V. (1998) *Counting girls out* (2nd edition). London: Falmer Press

Weber M. (1968) *Economy and Society*, [original 1925, *Wirtschaft und Gesellschaft*] (ed. Roth, G, and Wittich, C) NY: Bedminster Press

Welshman, J. (2006a) *The Cycle of Deprivation: myths and misconceptions.* London; Longview (accessed at http://www.longviewuk.com/pages/documents/PQcycle.pdf, 17 September 2010)

Welshman, J. (2006b) From the Cycle of Deprivation to Social Exclusion: Five Continuities. *The Political Quarterly*, 77, 4, pp 475-484

West, A. (2007) Poverty and educational attainment: why do families from low-income families tend to do less well at school? *Benefits,* 15, 3, pp 283 - 297

Whitty, G. (1974) Sociology and the problem of radical educational change, in Flude., M and Ahier, J. (eds) *Educability, Schools and Ideology*, London: Croom Helm

Wilkinson, R and Pickett, K. (2009) T*he Spirit Level: Why equal societies almost always do better.* London: Allen Lane

Wilkinson, W. (2009) Thinking Clearly about Economic Inequality. *Policy Analysis* 640 (Washington DC: Cato Institute)

Willey, R. (2010) *Brewer's Dictionary of London Phrase and Fable.* London: Chambers

Williams R (1961) *The Long Revolution.* London: Chatto and Windus

Willms, D. (1999) Quality and Inequality in Children's Literacy: the effects of families, schools and communities. in Keating, D. and Hertzman, C. (eds) *Developmental Health and the Wealth of Nations.* New York: Guilford

Wollstonecraft, M., (1792, 2009) *A Vindication of the Rights of Woman.* (ed Lynch, D., 3rd ed). New York: Norton

World Bank (2005) *World Development Report 2006: Equity and Development* Washington DC: The International Bank for Reconstruction and Development / The World Bank

World Bank (2006) *Summary of ediscussion (Part II): Does Inequality Matter?* (accessed at http://web.worldbank.org/WBSITE/EXTERNAL/EXTDEC/EXTRESE ARCH/EXTWDRS/EXTWDR2006/0,,contentMDK:20279721~pageP K:64167689~piPK:64167673~theSitePK:477642,00.html#question_1, 27 June 2011

Young, M. (1958) *The Rise of the Meritocracy.* London: Thames and Hudson

—. (1971) *Knowledge and Control* . London: Collier Macmillan

—. (2001) Down with Meritocracy. *The Guardian*, Friday 29 June 2001

Ziegler, E., Kagan, S. L. and Hall, N. (eds) (1996) *Children, Families and Government: Preparing for the Twenty-First Century.* New York: Cambridge University Press